Credo brings together essays written at different stages in Imants Tillers' career, from 'Locality Fails' (1982) to 'Journey to Nowhere' (2018), and closes with 'The Sources', commissioned for this collection, on the artists and writers who have influenced his work. Together, they offer both a personal credo, and a way of understanding the art and literature formed by the experience of migration. Tillers' concepts like 'the idea of incommensurability' and 'reversible destiny', his ideas about appropriation and the importance of reproduction in Australian culture, the encyclopaedic range of his work, and his orientation and re-orientation towards Aboriginal art, articulate an aesthetic which seeks connections between the local and the international, and a recognition of the complexities of provincialism.

Imants Tillers is one of Australia's most distinguished and innovative contemporary artists. He was born in Sydney in 1950, after his parents emigrated from Latvia as refugees. His first solo exhibition was at Watters Gallery in 1973. He has represented Australia at international exhibitions, such as the São Paulo Bienal (1975), Documenta 7 (1982) and the Venice Biennale (1986), and has been the subject of many individual exhibitions nationally and internationally. In 2006, the National Gallery of Australia hosted a retrospective of his work, *One world, many visions.* In 2018 the Latvian National Museum of Art in Riga honoured Tillers with the major retrospective *Journey to Nowhere.*

IMANTS TILLERS

CREDO

Published 2022
from the Writing and Society Research Centre
at Western Sydney University
by the Giramondo Publishing Company
PO Box 752
Artarmon NSW 1570 Australia
www.giramondopublishing.com

Designed by Jenny Grigg
Typeset by Andrew Davies
in Tiempos Regular 9/15pt

Printed and bound by Ligare Book Printers
Distributed in Australia by NewSouth Books

A catalogue record for this book is available from the National Library of Australia.

ISBN 978-1-922725-33-2

9 8 7 6 5 4 3 2 1

The Giramondo Publishing Company acknowledges the support of Western Sydney University in the implementation of its book publishing program.

This project has been assisted by the Commonwealth Government through the Australia Council, its arts funding and advisory body.

Contents

Preface

From Wassily Kandinsky's *Concerning the Spiritual in Art* (1911) to Joseph Kosuth's 'Art After Philosophy' (1969), artists have always been important contributors to the written discourse on art. The first essay in this selection, 'Locality Fails', was commissioned by Paul Taylor for an early issue of *Art+Text* in 1982, and the last, 'The Sources', by Ivor Indyk in 2019 for this collection, and is published here for the first time. Unlike the iconic and polemical texts of Kandinsky and Kosuth, which can stand alone as powerful manifestos of a particular time and place, this selection of essays has no overarching theme, no grand narrative. It is fragmentary in nature, with essays written for specific purposes – for magazines, for exhibition catalogues, for conferences, for lectures – these texts are akin to 'speeches delivered on just such and such an occasion'.[1]

Since I never envisaged these essays being collected in a single volume, overlaps occur. Indeed, from time to time I have quoted the same sources exactly, and so inevitably there are a number of repetitions. Instead of editing out these repetitions, I decided to keep them. For I am not afraid of 'repetition' – indeed repetition is one of the fundamentals, not only of my writing, but of my painting as well. Occasionally I have tried to make exact copies of my own pre-existing work. In my paintings, which combine text and image, there are several phrases which have been repeated so many times that I have forgotten their origin, and they now seem to emanate from my own body of work.

Without doubt the phrase that I have repeated the most is from the French symbolist poet, Stéphane Mallarmé: 'A Throw of the Dice will Never Abolish Chance.' Since 1998 this phrase has become something of a mantra for me – framing almost every painting I have executed. It speaks to me about some kind of profound truth in relation to 'chance' and 'destiny' – the essence of the mystery of our lives – the degree to which we *can* and *cannot* mould, influence or determine our life-trajectory. We well know that the unexpected can arrive at any moment, though fortunately not every life will end up as a shipwreck!

Therefore, just as 'quotation' and 'appropriation' are fundamental tenets of my work, so too is 'repetition'. Also, as Mallarmé once declared: 'All the Great masters, ancient and modern, plagiarized Homer, and Homer plagiarized God.'

1 Marcel Duchamp on how 'readymades' can be inscribed as 'readymades' only at a particular moment.

Locality Fails
1982

Albert Namatjira was born on 28 July 1902 (sharing a birthday with Marcel Duchamp born in 1887) in Hermannsburg, Central Australia. He was a member of the Aranda tribe and worked as a stockman, cameleer, and station hand at the Hermannsburg mission. There, after seeing an exhibition by Rex Battarbee and John Gardner in 1934, he attempted, untaught, drawings and pokerwork figures of animals and birds on wood not in the traditional manner of Aboriginal representation but in the style of Rex Battarbee. In 1936 on Battarbee's next visit to Central Australia, Namatjira offered his services as a cameleer in return for painting lessons. In imitating Battarbee's subjects, technique, and compositional preferences, Namatjira became the first Aboriginal artist to work in a characteristically non-Aboriginal manner, and for this accomplishment achieved a modicum of fame, as recorded in the 1950 edition of *Who's Who in Australia*.

In this volume, the most remarkable statement (even more remarkable than the Mission Superintendent's observation that Albert is 'happiest if sitting in sand or around a campfire, playing marbles like others of his tribe') is that his *recreation* is given as 'walk-about out bush'.[1] But while in 1950 'walk-abouts' were strictly 'recreational', in the 1970s they became 'avant-garde'. Though this was the case for British artists such as Richard Long and Hamish Fulton, rather than for Aboriginal artists.

Today, however, in Australia, the obvious distinctions between Long's 'art' and Namatjira's 'hobby' are becoming blurred, as more and more contemporary advantages are extracted from an association with 'Aboriginality'. In fact, the contemporary Australian art scene is now marked by two apparently convergent tendencies: the assimilation of 'traditional' Aboriginal cultural forms into 'contemporary' art and the emergence of 'Aboriginality' (in defiance of the dictionary definition) as a ubiquitous quality which is no longer the exclusive domain of 'black' Aboriginals.

The change in attitude towards 'traditional' Aboriginal art is most forcefully demonstrated by the inclusion of Aboriginal paintings (not as anthropological curiosities but as contemporary works in their own right) in recent exhibitions, such as the 1979 and 1982 Biennales of Sydney, and *Australian Perspecta 1981*. This acceptance of Aboriginal art can be attributed in part to the promotional activities of the Aboriginal Arts Board of the Australia Council, and organisations such as the Papunya Tula Artists cooperative which markets 'traditional' Aboriginal paintings done in 'modern' media, as well as the commercial success of private entrepreneurs in marketing ventures such as the *Gallery of Dreams* at Hogarth Gallery.[2]

However, the other more subtle and powerful reason for this acceptance is that certain forms in recent contemporary art seem to be convergent with Aboriginal art (and even 'lifestyle') to the extent that to a non-Aboriginal audience they have the atmosphere of 'Aboriginality'. This atmosphere may be evoked through references to aspects of a primitive lifestyle – to the look of its rituals, its artefacts and the natural environment in which they are perceived to occur. Thus in *Australian Perspecta 1981* the works of artists who were presumably influenced by or had an affinity with Aboriginal art were installed in the same space as the acrylic paintings of Clifford Possum Tjapaltjarri, Tim Leura

Tjapaltjarri, and Charlie Tjapangati. Ironically the 'Aboriginality' of this art could be seen to represent a reciprocal (white) position to Namatjira's 'European' watercolours.[3]

Despite its irrefutable presence, the new sense of 'Aboriginality' evades definition and even enunciation. It exists in the local work as a nuance, an inflection. For example, Bernice Murphy alludes to the incipient 'Aboriginality' in certain works in the following almost opaque way:

> The recent concern in art with the environment, archaeology and anthropology, and rehabilitation (through performance art) of the mythopoeic consciousness, personal symbols and a sense of generalised ritual is particularly important for the release and enrichment of new imaginative material into the bloodstream of Australian art.[4]

Robert Lindsay in the foreword to his exhibition, *Survey 15: Relics and Rituals* at the National Gallery of Victoria, is no more explicit. He suggests:

> It is the power and simplicity of communication which is inherent in totemic objects, archetypal images and tribal rituals, that the artist hopes will cut through the habits of contemporary sophisticated forms of communication. It is the return to fundamentals, the simple realities of life that through magic and mystification may evoke archetypal responses and emotions.[5]

Moreover, this strategy of nuance spans the entire range of contemporary art production in Australia, from formalist painting to radical socially engaged work, and even spills into the related areas of fashion and design. Thus lyrical abstractionists (or more recently neo-expressionists) desiring the aura of 'Aboriginality' shift their palettes (and titles) towards the 'desert' colours – the ochres, browns, and reds – but otherwise continue in their internationally derived styles as before.[6] The socially engaged artist on the other hand accrues 'Aboriginality' by association – by basing a performance, for example, on a pertinent Aboriginal issue (land rights) or by taking part in a collaborative photographic project with Aboriginals. An 'Aboriginal' inflection can be found in the most naive or the most sophisticated work – it does not matter whether the reference is serious (supporting their culture) or ironic in tone (exposing our in-built prejudices).

The reluctance for a more explicit identification with Aboriginals, for an authentic 'cultural convergence', can in part be explained by the deep guilt underlying Australian culture.[7] For the history of white settlement in Australia in relation to Aboriginals is a story of homicide, rape, the forcible abduction of children from their parents and the methodical dispossession of the lands upon which their wellbeing, self-respect, and survival have depended. 'Cultural convergence' is attractive as an *idea* because it offers a painless way to expiate our collective guilt for this history while simultaneously suggesting an easy solution to the more mundane but nevertheless pressing problem of finding a uniquely Australian content to our art in an international climate sympathetic to the notion of 'regional' art. The reality of 'cultural convergence', which necessitates that political and economic inequities be rectified first, is a less satisfying prospect. Certainly 'Aboriginality' is not a new idea – the Antipodeans in the 1950s and the Jindyworobak poets in the 1940s, as well as others before them like Margaret Preston (who suggested it should form the basis of a 'modern' Australian art), were attracted to it – the difference today is that contemporary art forms and media particularly in the areas of informal sculpture and performance can approximate more closely the 'look' of traditional Aboriginal artefacts, rituals, and environments.

The 'concerned conscience' about the Aboriginal people which 'Aboriginality' might reflect, however, does not often originate among the Australian-born. Interest in Aboriginal culture has and continues to come mostly from abroad.[8] (They do not have to share our guilt.) Thus during the Sydney Biennale *European Dialogue* (1979) Australian artists were often dismayed by the interest in and knowledge of Aboriginal culture shown by visiting artists and critics and the almost aggressive indifference they displayed to the Australian urban environment and its culture. Some, like Marina Abramović and Ulay even returned later (under a Visual Arts Board grant) to seek out (with typically Germanic zeal and determination) the Aboriginal influence for their own work. Their stay culminated in an 'alchemical' performance at the Art Gallery of New South Wales: *Gold Found by the Artists*. This work (dealing with their 'survival experience, perception changes, energy and telepathy') together with the attitudes subsequently expressed about Aboriginals, stands as a conspicuous model of a more 'serious', more earnest Aboriginality for local artists.[9] Since 'advanced' art in the twentieth century habitually aspires to the condition of religion, it is little wonder that the spiritual resources of Aboriginal culture and its esoteric practices should now be recognised, and association with it consciously sought.

Suzi Gablik, in an article for *Art in America* titled 'Report from

Australia', emphasises the links to the continent's Aboriginal past in certain contemporary work. She speaks of Australian artists being less embroiled in repressive cultural heritages than their American or European counterparts and thus able to look sympathetically to nature and even 'to trace, in a clear, quiet way, some old paths back to the aboriginal presence'.[10] Such optimistic remarks (as exhortations to action) clearly reflect the change in critical attitudes towards 'regionalism', a word that now has ascendancy over the formerly popular and derogatory expression 'provincialism'. For today we believe that 'remarkable work is as likely to arise in Cracow, Turin, Düsseldorf, Vienna, Paris, London or Amsterdam as in New York'.[11] Why not Sydney or Melbourne as well? The old Jindyworobak notion of *environmental value* – the 'slow moulding of all people within a continent or region towards the human form which that continent demands' – seems ready for a revival, and 'Aboriginality' is being offered again as an appropriate form.[12]

This widespread though largely unstated hope (or even belief) in an Indigenous Australian art ignores the contemporary understanding of the nature of the physical world. Just as the discovery of the special theory of relativity and quantum mechanics revolutionised our view of the world in the first quarter of the twentieth century, so Bell's theorem will revolutionise our view in the last quarter. In 1975, Henry Stapp, in a work supported by the US Energy Research and Development Administration, wrote 'Bell's theorem is the most profound discovery of science.'[13]

Bell's theorem shows that either the statistical predictions of quantum theory or 'the principle of local causes' is false. It does not say which one is false only that both of them cannot be true. When the Freedman-Clauser experiment confirmed that the statistical predictions of quantum theory were correct it proved that the principle of local causes was false. The important thing about Bell's theorem which makes it relevant to the present discussion is that it puts the dilemma posed by quantum phenomena clearly into the realm of macroscopic phenomena – it shows that our ordinary ideas about the world are somehow profoundly deficient even on a macroscopic level.[14]

And it does not matter how Bell's theorem is reformulated, it invariably projects the 'irrational' aspects of sub-atomic phenomena into the macroscopic domain. It says that not only do events in the realm of the very small behave in ways which are utterly different from our common sense view of the world, but that events in the world at large, the world of sports cars and freeways (or the world of pristine white walls and spilt drinks), also behave in such ways. Since Bell's theorem *proves* that the principle of local causes fails it is of crucial relevance to the present discussion of a 'local' content in Australian art, 'regionalism' and 'Aboriginality'.

The principle of local causes asserts that what happens in an area does not depend upon variables subject to the control of an experimenter in a distant 'space-like separated' area. The principle of local causes is common sense. The results of an experiment in a place distant and 'space-like separated' should not depend on what we decide to do right here. Thus, it is assumed, 'local' art inevitably reflects 'local' conditions. Local conditions might include the continuation of an Aboriginal presence in Australia but equally they might include the transference of art information and models from New York to Sydney. For New York and Sydney are not 'space-like separated' at all: information is transmitted through identifiable channels (i.e. mechanical reproductions in aeroplanes) and thus arrives not mysteriously but by identifiable means. Could it be otherwise!

According to Bell's theorem it *is* otherwise. For the failure of the principle of local causes implies that there can be unexplained connectedness between events in different 'space-like separated' places and that this connectedness allows, for example, an experimenter (e.g. an artist) in one place to affect the state of a system in another remote (apparently unconnected) place. Or this can happen in reverse. Thus to take an almost preposterous example, Böcklin's painting *The Island of the Dead*, completed in 1880 in Munich, might be the direct (though slightly delayed) result of the attempted extermination of the Aboriginal Tasmanians by the white settlers, despite the fact that Böcklin would have had no direct knowledge of this catastrophic event.[15] (Like the mother who rose in alarm at the same instant that her daughter's distant automobile crashed into a tree.) Bell's theorem would imply that this is not merely an association nor a matter of 'pure chance':

> ...the conversion of potentialities into actualities cannot proceed on the basis of locally available information. If one accepts the usual ideas about how information propagates through space and time, then Bell's Theorem shows that the macroscopic responses cannot be independent of far-away causes. This problem is neither resolved nor alleviated by saying that the response is determined by 'pure chance', Bell's Theorem proves precisely that the determination of the macroscopic response must be 'nonchance', at least to the extent of allowing some sort of dependence of this response upon the far-away cause.[16]

While it is outside the scope of this chapter to pursue the implications of Bell's theorem on contemporary Australian art in any greater detail, it suffices to suggest that the conscious striving after the appearance of 'localness' could be an utterly futile and nonsensical activity, except in that it might produce effects (unknown to us) in other, remote 'space-like separated' regions (say in the Carpathian Mountains or the Upper Urals).

The failure of the principle of local causes also invites speculation on the 'distant' origins of 'local' phenomena. How are we to interpret the fact that objects no more convincing than the crude representations in Giorgio de Chirico's paintings occur with an unnatural frequency in the Australian suburban landscape? Does the mere resemblance of these dissociated, displaced objects to those in de Chirico's pictures necessarily imply a causal connection?

In fact these objects can be explained by more conventional and immediate causes. After all they are not so surprising in themselves considering the degree to which Australian experience is mediated by photography and photographic reproductions. For these objects which seem to be the members of an entirely new *species of object* are derived (mutated) from photographs though they are not photographs in themselves. While often resembling houses (master-built project homes) at other times they can resemble the Greek temples of de Chirico's pictures. What is common to these objects is that some essential property seems to be missing. Collaged together from prefabricated components (often neo-classical in their reference) chosen from printed brochures, their visual attributes can be best described as 'flatness', 'frontality', 'sharp focus', 'full colour', 'high resolution', etc. In real life they evoke strong feelings of déjà vu, and in the presence of other such objects (e.g. in a street) they seem to partake of a game of quotation and cross-reference. Their most plausible attribute is that of being photogenic. Also since they are entirely derived from photographic representations they have the same qualities of surface, of reproducibility, and they acknowledge the same formal devices of framing and cropping as do photographs themselves.[17]

A conventional and plausible explanation (pre-Bell's theorem) of the resemblance between these objects and the images in certain of de Chirico's paintings would point to the fact that 'simulation' (the quintessential quality of Australian life and culture and the means by which these objects arise) is also an abiding interest of de Chirico – particularly in his later work. In these unfashionable works, the melancholy of *places* (of deserted Italian piazzas on autumn afternoons) yields to the melancholy of his own personal metaphysical situation. This is expressed in a twofold strategy of simulation: on the one hand 'precise variations' on his early 'metaphysical' works, and on the other hand an almost inept imitation of 'traditional' painting and its subject matter. (Simulation invariably allows the simultaneous embrace of apparently contradictory positions since the 'surface' is borrowed from 'elsewhere' and does not necessarily reflect real intentions or meanings.)

De Chirico claimed 'Pictor classicus sum' (I am a classical painter) and painted classical subjects in the classical manner.[18] He even painted portraits of himself and his wife in seventeenth-century costume. These paintings reflect an almost pathological nostalgia – a 'quixotic' desire to defy the incontrovertible circumstances of his 'time and place' – and there is in this echoes of the recent Australian experience (post-1788). But whereas de Chirico's later work, in the intensity of its anguish, bears comparison with the work of Francis Bacon or Hermann Nitsch, Australian simulation (except for unintentional, largely architectural manifestations) is bound to a comfortable mediocrity by its own tentativeness. We do not yet have a *white* artist who can declare with conviction: 'I am Aboriginal.'

But while these connections and associations between de Chirico's interests and the Australian experience conform to the commonsense view of the world (of the pervasiveness of 'local' phenomena), how are we to interpret the presence of *this* fragment of a place called 'Melbourne' (circa 1929) mapped into the second sentence of de Chirico's novel *Hebdomeros*:

> And then began the tour of that strange building situated in a street that looked forbidding, although it was distinguished and not gloomy. As seen from the street the building was reminiscent of a German consulate in Melbourne. Its ground floor was entirely taken up with large stores. Although it was neither Sunday nor a holiday, the stores were closed, endowing this part of the street with an air of tedium and melancholy, a certain desolation, that particular atmosphere which pervades Anglo-Saxon towns on Sundays.[19]

Luckily a world in which 'locality fails' is far more interesting than the one in which we are limited to our immediate circumstances and which we are suffered upon to reflect in our art.

Notes

1 J.A. Alexander (ed.) (1950) *Who's Who in Australia*, Sydney, p. 530.

2 The contemporary 'look' and practicality of these works in contrast to the sand-paintings from which they are derived makes them fit more easily into the contemporary context.

3 In the Biennale of Sydney *Visions of Disbelief* (1982), an Aboriginal sand-painting (not 'simulations' of sand-painting as in the previous biennale) was given an entire space to itself, thereby endowing this work with a pivotal significance.

4 Bernice Murphy (1981) *Australian Perspecta* (catalogue), p. 13.

5 Robert Lindsay (1981) *Survey 15: Relics & Rituals* (catalogue), National Gallery of Victoria.

6 This is in direct contrast to Aboriginal painters themselves whose choice of colours is limited by local availability of certain pigments rather than being inherently 'Aboriginal' colour preferences. Thus prior to the 1977 exhibition of Papunya art works at Realities Gallery in Melbourne, the Aboriginal artists wished to add to the intended purchase of acrylics some blue, green, and possibly other colours for use in their work. However, they were talked out of this by a white artist's advice to stick to their 'traditional' range of pigments. (See Dismas M. Zika (1981) *Landscape, Some Interpretations* (catalogue), Tasmanian School of Art.) The idea of extending the colour range could be seen as the same kind of cultural adaptation as, say, the substitution of readily available 'galiron' sheets for 'traditional' though scarce stringybark as a building material.

7 Bernard Smith (1980) *The Spectre of Truganini*, Sydney: Boyer Lectures, ABC, pp. 44–52.

8 Ibid., p. 27.

9 Jennifer Phipps (1981) 'Marina Abramovic/Ulay', *Art & Text* 3: 45, 46–50.

10 Suzi Gablik (January 1981) 'Report from Australia', *Art in America*: 29.

11 Nick Waterlow (1979) *European Dialogue: A Commentary* (catalogue), Biennale of Sydney.

12 Les Murray (1977) 'The human-hair thread', *Meanjin*, Aboriginal issue, 36, 4: 569

13 Henry Stapp (1975) 'Bell's Theorem and world process', *Il Nuovo Cimento*, 298: 191

14 Henry Stapp (1971) 'S-Matrix interpretation of quantum theory', *Physical Review*, D3: 1303ff.

15 Truganini, the last of the original Tasmanian Aboriginals, died in 1876.

16 Stapp, 'S-Matrix interpretation', op. cit.

17 See Paul Taylor's catalogue essay in (1982) *Eureka: Artists from Australia*, London: Institute of Contemporary Arts and Serpentine Gallery.

18 *De Chirico* (1968), New York: Harry Abrams p. 13.

19 Ibid. p. 13.

Reprinted from Art & Text 6, *Melbourne, 1982, and published in this volume by kind permission of the editors.*

Fear of Texture
1983

I had off nex day no digging to do only in my head for Nex Nite and my connexion. I had a nuff and moren a nuff to connect with all I had to do wer sort it out my head wer perwel humming and spinning with it.
Russell Hoban, *Riddley Walker*[1]

...I think and think and think and then I paint around the think which seems to sort of ring some sort of bell somewhere inside my head. It's almost like that.
John Firth-Smith[2]

Art in Australia is about to get thicker. Miles and miles of canvas are to be unfurled and acres of thick impasto paint are to be scraped and scumbled by thousands of Antipodean 'Art Ants' galvanised into a frenzied collective action.[3] It is as though the precariously flat and provisional surface of Australian art up to now is about to be given some 'depth' and integrity by the extrusion of tonnes of paint, spread evenly to a 'meaty' consistency over an exponentially expanding area.

The recent appearance of a promotional package from the Australian paint manufacturer Chromacryl anticipates, if it does not 'pre-create', this reality. Addressed nationally to *Painting Department* it includes:

One small piece of canvas with heavily applied Atelier Impasto Acrylic.
Reproduction from [an insert in] March issue of *Art and Australia* showing one of the first acrylic 'oil' paintings by Michael Johnson.

The accompanying letter explains how this NEW FORMULATION HIGH DENSITY PAINTERLY ACRYLIC (NFHDPA) is not 'doctored' with gel medium but has naturally the 'body of oils'. The caption to the reproduced painting describes the medium as 'atelier on canvas'. The accompanying technical notes stress that Atelier has all the desired qualities of oil paint – its 'tactile meaty impasto' quality, its 'sharp definition', its retention of the 'vitality of gesture' – and yet has all the practical advantages of acrylic paint, notably those of working speed and versatility. The technical emphasis throughout is that *Atelier looks like oil paint*.

Thus market research has already caught up with the local 'zeitgeist' – the semblance of expressionist painting, the return to figuration, the return to oil paint and the necessity of texture. This new acrylic paint has been specially formulated for local conditions but, conceived in a 'popist' spirit, it ignores 'sincerity' (a quality which is exclusively and inextricably embedded in the use and even the smell of oil paint) and aims for the mere *simulation* of the 'look' of oil paint. It also attempts to interpolate its brand name, Atelier, as a common noun like 'xerox' into the vocabulary of common usage.

The painting by Michael Johnson, in Chromacryl's reproduction, with its flattened though still conspicuous texture, is the paradigm of the 'photo-ready' work – a work produced solely for the purposes of being reproduced and which has no necessary existence beyond the photographic reproduction. This reproduction, however, is not inside the body of *Art and Australia* for long, but is inserted into its ideological space as 'loose-leaf' and 'detachable', and is quick to make its get-away after committing an act of terrorism. The makers of Atelier acrylic 'oil' paint attempt to seduce those painters nervous about the new spirit in painting to change their brand while they, the manufacturers, pursue their own aesthetic and ideological goals. There is little doubt that Atelier NFHDPA will be the prosaic and ironic art substance of the 1980s, leaving 'experimental' and 'post-object' substances such as Nu-Art fixative spray far behind.

Questions of 'finish' have always been of crucial importance in Australian art – a fact clearly recognised by the makers of Atelier. Thus Margaret Plant has pointed out that it was 'finish' that divided local Melbourne artists in 1977, rather than stylistic issues such as figuration versus abstraction or neo-realism versus conceptualism. Her argument about 'finish', however, was aimed primarily at the 'abstract-expressionist' painters, and she described their offerings as suave, generously-scaled and decorative, and 'in the absence of aggression and a sense of challenge to the style in which they work, they have consolidated an audience and declared themselves as the rear-garde.'[4]

Fred Cress, after his popular show at Powell Street Gallery in 1976, was singled out for particular attention:

> The paintings operated with a careful and established set of apparently rough effects, calculated to give a spontaneous impression. Such effects – dribbles, asymmetrical patches of colour, lyrical hues, colour close-keyed in tone, contrasts from canvas to canvas to convey a variety and contrast of moods – look to be the marks of a spontaneous painter but in fact have become the agents of over-finish.'[5]

By way of contrast, Plant referred to the Melbourne painters of the

1940s (whose revival in 1977 was yet to take place) – Boyd, Tucker, Perceval – remarking positively on their 'turgid colour, muddied with turpentine' and their 'hasty and impatient' application of paint, adding that such marks of an ill-refined style could be construed as positive qualities serving the urgency of wartime subject matter.

The very absence of traditional skills, of modelling, of care and clarity become virtues carrying moral connotations of urgent honesty. Some thirty to forty years later these paintings strike us as authentic images of a modern and local evil marked by a genuineness of style.[6]

However, the differences between the expressionists of the 1940s and the 'abstract-expressionists' of the 1970s which were clearly evident in 1977 are no longer so. And ironically the reason for this blending of two opposed attitudes is that in 1983 the significantly textured surface has displaced the thickly smeared one as a signifier carrying 'moral connotations of urgent honesty'. The 'neo-expressionist' painting of Peter Booth, for example, is central to the reconciliation of this paradox. When Booth switched from his abstract style of the late 1960s and early 1970s to a personal form of figurative expressionism in 1976, he brought to it the elegant repertoire of formal qualities he had skilfully utilised in his abstract work; this included his preferred palette of brown, ochre, red, black, a generous sense of scale and a refined sense of 'finish'. His abstract paintings just prior to this radical shift had moved from the austerity of his earlier works to 'the melodrama of gaudy canvases with thick palette-knifed paint and gouaches, with the paper bending with the weight of pigment.'[7] It was this 'thick palette-knifed paint' in particular that Booth retained in his new expressive, figurative work.

Ever since Booth's work changed from abstraction to figuration it has been widely, almost systematically, linked to the work of the expressionists of the 1940s. Thus Leon Paroissien echoes Nancy Underhill in confirming this link, stating that there were certain Australian models for Booth, 'those Australian painters who from the late 1930s and early 1940s conveyed their highly personal responses to the distinctive environment and space of their country – Arthur Boyd, John Perceval, Sidney Nolan, Albert Tucker and Danila Vassilieff'.[8]

The obvious contrasts of 'finish', however, are ignored and Booth's 'thick palette-knifed' paint is imbued with 'moral connotations of urgent honesty' by appealing to the sincerity and honesty of Booth himself. It is lazily assumed that Booth arrived at figuration from abstraction independently of such shifts occurring simultaneously in other countries, and that the 'darkly expressive' tendencies had always been present in his abstract work.[9] This is the means by which a certain texture has become the new *moral sign* in Australian painting in the 1980s. The manufacturers of Atelier are well prepared.

While it is now comparatively easy for young Australian artists without an existing artistic history to partake of this burgeoning 'regional' tradition, it is still more difficult for the formerly 'modernist' abstract painters of the 1960s and 1970s to do likewise without compromising their integrity with an unabashed display of opportunism. However, they can at least shift their work in the relevant direction by employing certain aspects of the exemplary model provided by Booth and others. Thus in 1983, Fred Cress showed paintings at the Macquarie Galleries in Sydney in which the paint was appreciably thicker and in which the 'spontaneous' drips of bygone days had been displaced by expressive brushwork. Also, the paintings had become more ambiguous and were no longer entirely abstract or 'all-over'. In some a triangulated motif (suggesting a biomorphic or architectural form) dominated on a receding 'ground'. The palette had also changed, becoming more 'ominous' in its preference for blacks, reds and greys, and in some works there were even zigzags.[10] These elegant paintings, like those of the complicit English artist John Walker (now resident in Australia), hovered somewhere *between* figuration and abstraction, but in conforming to the new demands of acceptable 'finish' they seemed to be participating in this new spirit in painting.

It is clear that Australian 'neo-expressionism' and its related manifestations attempt to stress integrity and authenticity over irony and ambivalence. It also attempts to establish a sympathetic identification with its expressionist forebears rather than merely pillaging from them as part of a general strategy of stylistic quotation. In these features, and in emphasising individual and historical stylistic continuities over discontinuities, it is unworthy of comparison with the most significant work overseas to which it is nevertheless being compared.

Our local conception of 'neo-expressionism' does not seem to take into account the apt description of European and American counterparts as 'perceptually oscillating between mutually incompatible attitudes or theories',[11] nor that it is sometimes referred to as 'post-conceptual', nor even that it shares common attitudes (for example, the idea of 'pre-created experience') and common strategies ('quotation' and 'simulation') with the trend, which in Australia it is seen to oppose – that is to say, 'un-expressionism'.[12]

'Neo-expressionism' in Europe and America employs inevitably a far wider textural range (both thicker *and* thinner) in its paintings than is generally found here. For example, to consider the thick end of the scale, in Australia we have not encountered anything comparable to the bitumen, sand and straw mixed in with Anselm Kiefer's dense oil paint, nor the sheets of lead, iron tools and burnt logs supported by his paint surface; nor Julian Schnabel's giant figures sketched in broom-sized brushstrokes on canvases primed with a bed of broken plates. These literal demonstrations of *how to paint with a hammer* starkly contrast with our reticent use of the palette-knife.[13] Our acceptable textural range is too easily *defined* by 'atelier'.

Who can forget the public indignation surrounding the purchase of Jackson Pollock's *Blue Poles* by the Australian National Gallery in 1975 for $1.3 million. The popular press ran sensationally embellished stories about how Pollock had painted *Blue Poles* in a drunken orgy with his semi-conscious cronies lending a helping hand (or foot), staggering around ankle-deep in paint and urine which was afloat with broken glass and cigarette butts. (This popular Antipodean image of the spontaneous gesture was a far cry from the simplified transcriptions of our local 'abstract-expressionists' who turned this style into such a popular form of interior décor in the 1960s and 1970s.) Since the opening of the Australian National Gallery in October 1982, we can scrutinise the surface of *Blue Poles* directly and its 'flatness' is a revelation to us – the offensive fragment of broken glass protrudes not more than half a centimetre. It is as though our dislocation from the work up till now, since previously it was only available in reproduced form, hid a horrendous truth.

Perhaps what is lost in the mechanical reproduction of the work of art is not only the 'aura' of the original but also the tactile qualities of its surface. In Australia, our knowledge and experience of art has until recently been almost entirely in this mediated form: the variety of available textures of art have all been mapped onto the same smooth glossy paper and this surface has become our collective surrogate experience for that of the originals. We have thus become anaesthetised to texture. As a consequence, it is those very tactile qualities which reproduction suppresses that we magnify and distort in our imaginations – hence our fear of texture. This also explains the conservative textural range in that contemporary painting which seeks to be 'ominous', 'magical', 'garish', 'sinister', 'dislocated', 'harsh', 'bizarre', 'gaudy', 'evil' but above all *'genuine'*.[14]

Fortunately, in Australian art there are still some tendencies to deviate from this prescribed textural norm and many of those artists willing to deviate have taken refuge in the *dematerialisation of texture* which the dot-screen permits – i.e. in the reproduction of the reproduction or in allied photographic processes. There is however also another alternative 'dot-screen' which unlike the precise and rigid screen of mechanical and electronic reproduction is 'degenerated' in its structure, and even resembles at times the planometric view of our semi-arid interior, seen from high above as an eminently flat ground punctuated only by the sporadic and unfocused dotting of scrubby mallees. This is the literal though abstracted image of the Australian landscape as presented to us in some of Fred Williams' paintings but it is also the 'view' implied in some entirely abstract works – for example those of Ralph Balson or more recently Gunter Christmann. This 'dot-screen' structure however is most apparent in the works of the artists of Central Australia and the Western Desert who form the Papunya school of painters – artists such as Tim Leura Tjapaltjarri, Clifford Possum Tjapaltjarri, Uta Uta Tjangala, Charlie Tjapangati, Turkey Tolson Tjupurrula and Mick Namarari Tjapaltjarri and others.[15]

Recently it was suggested that painting might be thought of *not* in terms of a finite object but as a property of a continuous surface existing in time ad infinitum. 'I propose that painting be thought of as an enormous roll of diversified fabric woven in a single piece and unrolled in time and space. This surface extends for miles and miles but never appears on display. Its continuity is interrupted and broken up – cut into – to form innumerable fragments and portions of canvas (paintings), creating intervals and separations the understanding of which could greatly influence our way of thinking about and seeing painting, or for that matter continuity in the history of painting.'[16]

The truth of this proposition is clearly evident if we look at a room full of Papunya paintings. The initial impression, that each individual canvas is literally a fragment cut from the same cloth, is in fact so overwhelming that it is only with the familiarity that comes from concerted and extended study that we begin to detect a whole range of pertinent differences between paintings. What unifies this body of work so dramatically is the pervasiveness of the 'dot-screen'.

In Papunya painting, even though the 'dot-screen' is placed *over* the image, it tends to be a supple grid and thus accommodates and even defines the designs of the image below. Nevertheless because of the size of the dots and their continuity over the entire surface as a 'field' they tend to break down the image at the same instant as they define it: pictorial reality does not materialise out of the fusion of dots (as it does in mechanical and electronic reproduction techniques), rather it dissipates (like an after-image or hallucination) into a cloud of dots. Because of the immediacy of this purely optical effect, the dot-screen in Papunya painting frees the image from the materialism of texture. In this way, the dot-screen becomes the *image of dematerialisation*.

Papunya paintings have a very strong conceptual aspect and in several ways can be identified with the dematerialised aspects of the Australian conceptual art of the early 1970s. Firstly, Papunya paintings function as 'mnemonics for the stories which are sung and which comprise Aboriginal lore and law and they are also cartographic mnemonics which inform and remind them of topography and proprietary rights to land according to Aboriginal law.[17]

Since these paintings originally existed in the ephemeral form of ground-paintings, but now exist in the permanent form of paint on canvas, and are therefore coextensive and in competition with *other* conventional forms of painting, they could be described as 'post-conceptual': the word made flesh.

Ironically, unlike the haptic anaesthesia of 'palette-knifed' expressionism (which conforms to the prescriptive textural limits of the paint manufacturers, who recognised the existence of limits in the trajectory of recent painting, and defined and concretised them), the Papunya painters' relationship to their 'conceptual' painting – their image of dematerialisation (the dot-screen) – is emphatically tactile. Thus the painters, in explaining the significance of a painting, will touch the painted surface and follow the tracks to the sites represented with the sensitivity of blind men reading braille. It is interesting that the dematerialised Australian art of the early 1970s, while it privileged the 'conceptual' over the 'visual', was never entirely 'mental', rather it shifted the emphasis away from the purely visual (corrupted) sensory mode to the other sensory modes (the auditory, haptic, olfactory, kinaesthetic, etc.) in an attempt to re-purify optical vision. Thus in 1970 when Ian Milliss's celebrated piece *Walk Along This Line* (a length of masking tape installed on the floor, parallel and close to a wall with this title/instruction letrasetted on it) was shown in the Transfield Prize in Sydney and described as 'conceptual', the artist rightly disputed the claim, pointing out that its purpose was to bring into play (in Art) the little-used balance mechanism located in the middle ear. Considering that the first canvasboards were done in 1970–71, Papunya painting shares exactly the same historical period in Australia as conceptual art. Yet it was only in the latter part of this decade, when Tim Johnson as a conceptualist became one of Papunya painting's chief publicists, that these two eminently compatible artistic moments came together.

The dot-screen was not always present in Papunya painting. In fact, it appeared only *after* a major crisis in the history of Papunya painting. Initially, when Geoff Bardon encouraged the transposition of traditional Central Australian and Western Desert art from ground-painting or sand-painting onto canvas, the Aboriginal artists depicted their ritual figures, animals, people and mythological ancestors without any censorship, since the work was not painted for sale but for the pleasure of the activity and the recalled events and lore.[18] At first these images were painted on darkly primed backgrounds and there were hardly any dots to be seen in these paintings at all. However, when the work began to sell, the art changed. Other Aboriginal people saw the work on display and were angered by what seemed to be a blatant display of certain aspects of the secret-sacred men's world:

Almost overnight as it were all detailed depictions of human figures, sacred and other 'dangerous' aspects, were removed or modified in shape. In a related reaction backgrounds began to be painted-in rather than left stark. Patterns of straight lines, arcs and hatching were common at first, but this soon changed to dots, thus eliminating elements used on some sacred objects. Although dots are part of some sacred paintings, they are rarely in themselves more than very generally significant, whereas arcs and barred lines have a strong association with certain sacred elements.[19]

Thus the dot-screen appeared to fill the gap left by the sudden and traumatic withdrawal of the secret-sacred designs and images from the paintings. Now that he is aware of the possibility of the observation, appropriation and reproducibility of his sacred imagery by whites, the Papunya painter instead paints the 'pretty picture' or the 'easy story' – a satisfactory and true enough explanation but not a deep 'law' story. The dot-screen in Papunya painting is thus, in addition to any other significance, a sign of not just the radical and transcendent superficiality of this art but also of its *invisibility*.[20] There is a supreme irony in this since it is an attitude convergent with the art of 'White Aboriginals' – the Australian 'unexpressionists' – those who embrace the 'dot-screen' of mechanical reproduction either directly or through its agent, photography.[21]

An image with no texture is the apparition.

In 1982 John Young was using a procedure in which he would allow the camera to take its own picture. One such experiment produced a remarkable image: in a photograph taken in the Malevich room of the Stedelijk Museum in Amsterdam, one of Malevich's Suprematist crosses appears reflected like a mirage on the floor of the room. This effect is the result of the camera having its automatic delayed shutter-release mechanism activated and then being placed 'blindly', and thus by chance, on a metal railing at exactly the right point from which to create this illusion. Placed anywhere else but at this precise point and the illusion would have been broken. This result, like the occurrence of 'spontaneous images' on film, seems to be an 'unconsciously structured' event.[22]

An even more remarkable example of 'unaccountable' optical effects on photographs is to be found in a particular photograph taken by two Americans – Richard and Fred Veilleux of Waterville, Maine. When they took a photograph in their kitchen in July 1968 and developed the film they found a 'spontaneous image' superimposed over it. The image was later identified as an Australian Wandjina rock painting. There is an interesting footnote to this case. After the image had been described by Professor Charles Lyle as a 'pagan Last Supper' it was revealed that the image that the rock painting *obscured* in the photograph of the kitchen was a print of Leonardo's *The Last Supper,* which had been pinned to the wall.[23] This spontaneous superimposition is an ironic reversal when we consider the 'muscular Christianity' imposed on certain groups of Aboriginals after white contact.

It is not wise however to put too much trust in these 'apparitions' for in the desert mirages are dangerous – encouraging false hopes. Nevertheless, while we are condemned eternally to subsist on the arid surface of this *Island of the Dead*, and before we acquiesce in the apocalypse of impasto and simulated expression, we should reclaim the dot-screen and restore this 'cut-out portion of the fabric' back within the 'body' of modern Australian art.

Notes

1 Russell Hoban, *Riddley Walker* (London: Picador, 1980), p. 52.

2 Artist's Statement, *Survey 16* (catalogue, National Gallery of Victoria, 1981).

3 As the title of Sigmar Polke's celebrated painting *Higher Beings Command: Paint the Upper Right Corner Black* (1969) suggests, this is neither a unique nor local phenomenon.

4 Margaret Plant, 'Quattrocento Melbourne: Aspects of Finish 1973–1977' in *Studies in Australian Art* (University of Melbourne, 1978).

5 Ibid., p. 102.

6 Ibid., p. 100.

7 Ibid.

8 Leon Paroissien, 'Report from Sydney, The Fourth Biennale', *Art in America* (February 1983), p. 27.

9 Paul Taylor, 'Angst In My Pants', *Art & Text,* no. 7 (Spring 1982), pp. 56–7.

10 The use of the zigzag as an apocalyptic sign of contemporaneity seems confined to Australia, but here it is as ubiquitous as Banksia Speciosa.

11 Craig Owens, 'Honor, Power and the Love of Women', *Art in America* (January 1983), p. 9.

12 Germano Celant, 'From Alpha-Trainer to Subway', *Art & Text,* no. 9 (Autumn 1983), p. 65.

13 From Ian McKeever's exhibition *Black and White...or How to Paint With a Hammer* (London: Matt's Gallery, 1982).

14 All from Memory Holloway, *Young Melbourne Painters* (catalogue) (Melbourne: Monash University, 1982).

15 A 'degenerated' dot-screen is also *unconsciously* present in the work of certain younger artists where it is not the primary feature but is subordinated to other more conscious intentions. For example one thinks of the 'dot-screen' composed of pollen-grains in Peter Cripps' constructions *Film Phenomena* (1982) or Peter Tyndall's 'molecular' brushwork in his monochromatic series of paintings titled *detail, A Person Looks at a Work of Art / someone looks at something* (1976–1979). There is also John Young's constructivist chalk drawing on sandpaper which is not only 'molecular' (because of the grid of sand grains on the paper) but in which the image is 'carved' in reverse (by the absence of chalk) and resembles unintentionally an Aboriginal rock-engraving. The 'dot-screen' structure is used in Marianne Baillieu's paintings of 'angels' – each 'angel' however as a palpable and formless 'glob' of paint (one tube of paint per angel) in its gross materiality contradicts its spiritual aspirations. And in Tony Clark's paintings of classical temple plans, the columns become dots forming a screen more akin to Papunya painting than to the classical architectural traditions from which they are derived.

16 Germano Celant, 'Framed: Innocence or Gilt?', *Artforum* (Summer 1982), p. 49, reitering Deleuze and Guattari's *Mille Plateau.*

17 Andrew Crocker, 'Mr Sandman Bring Me a Dream', Papunya Tula Artists Pty Ltd, (Alice Springs 1981).

18 See Geoffrey Bardon, *Aboriginal Art of the Western Desert* (Adelaide: Rigby, 1969).

19 R.J. Kimber, *'Mr Sandman Bring Me a Dream'*, Papunya Tula Artists Pty Ltd (Alice Springs 1981).

20 'Invisibility' has been a common and successful artistic strategy in the art of the twentieth century. Most recently critical attention has focused on the late works of De Chirico (executed between 1950–1962), particularly those which were thought to be the most 'invisible' of all – the precise (manual) quotations of certain earlier metaphysical paintings. See Achille Bonito Oliva's *Warhol verso de Chirico* (catalogue) (Rome 1982).

21 See Paul Taylor, 'Popism – The Art of White Aborigines', *On the Beach,* No. 1 Autumn 1983, p. 30 and *Flash Art*, May 1983.

22 See also Tim Johnson's book *Coincidence* (1974 Sydney).

23 John Michell, Robert J.M. Rickard *Phenomena* (Thames & Hudson, 1977), frontispiece.

Reprinted from Art & Text 10, *Melbourne, 1983, and published in this volume by kind permission of the editors.*

In Perpetual Mourning
1984

Australia is the dumping ground for the rubbish of all the earth.
The Skull (Ross May)

In Australia the experience of works of art through mechanical reproduction always precedes their direct experience. For example, Enzo Cucchi's painting, *The Wind of the Black Roosters* (1982) bought recently by the Australian National Gallery, was reproduced in *Flash Art* before it could be seen firsthand in Canberra.[1] The caption 'Courtesy Canberra Museum', however, seemed to deny the reality of the Australian National Gallery banishing Cucchi's masterpiece (if it has to be in Australia) to an entirely fictitious repository of art. For Australians too, there is some comfort in this oversight – for the acknowledged presence of a Cucchi in Australia would evoke feelings of disbelief. It would undermine our sense of protection from 'originals' – from their aura, their surface and their authority. The dot-screen of mechanical reproduction renders all images equivalent, interchangeable, scale-less and surface-less; but above all, it makes them far more susceptible to local readings. Thus another of Cucchi's works in reproduction, *Fierce Painting* (1981), strangely echoes the distinctive profile of Jørn Utzon's Sydney Opera House; and we all recognise his desolate 'barbaric landscapes', not as prophetic images of the future, but as the severely eroded landscape of Australia's present.[2]

On 15 August 1983, the *Sydney Morning Herald* carried the following report:

Jackson Pollock's *Blue Poles* was reproduced in New York recently to mark the 27th anniversary of Pollock's death. Artist Mike Bidlo recreated the work on 132 masonite tiles and then gave them away to onlookers. Asked why he chose *Blue Poles*, Bidlo claimed that the canvas had helped change the Government of Australia. When the Australian people found out what the Government had paid for it, they were outraged. They threw the Government out! Pollock's painting was bought for $1.3 million by the Whitlam Government in 1973.

This report is remarkable for two reasons, the supreme almost mystical power it attributes to a work of art (the power to change governments), and the inversion of the normal state of affairs – that of artists outside of Australia 'recreating' works of art that are here.

Indeed the aura surrounding *Blue Poles* is such that even when attempting to talk about any other work, say for example, Shusaku Arakawa's painting *Out of Distance/Out of Texture* (1978), which is also on display in the Australian National Gallery, it is difficult not to mention Pollock's masterpiece. *Blue Poles* with its latticework of paint seems to act as a vortex into which all other works are drawn. Thus we cannot avoid seeing Arakawa's painting as the accumulation of a series of superimposed layers of paint. One layer is in the form of a text, another in the form of perspective lines, another in the form of an architectural plan (a living room) and yet another in the form of rotating lines which appear to be forming themselves into volumes (broken columns) which might even be the tentative visualisations of the point of consciousness. There may even be other layers. The rather mechanical construction of these layers in Arakawa's work, however, is in direct contrast to the loose intertwining of gestural, gossamer-like threads of paint in *Blue Poles*.

Or we might consider New Zealand artist Colin McCahon's painting *Victory Over Death 2* (1970), in which the starkly monochromatic and monumental typography of the words 'I AM' seems to echo New Zealand's mountainous topography. This reading of McCahon's painting is determined by our realisation that *Blue Poles*'s viewpoint is aerial and flat (like the viewpoint in Papunya painting) and echoes the enormous expanses of Australia's interior – its shifting veils of turbulence seen from high above, hypnotic and unfocused, through dust and haze.[3]

Cucchi's *The Wind of the Black Roosters* no doubt will eventually take its place in orbit as yet another satellite of *Blue Poles*, and its meaning, too, will be altered and overlaid by the meanings that emanate from this haloed fragment of 'modernism' which sits uncomfortably here on the other side of the earth. Like the sole surviving fragment of Western culture in Russell Hoban's apocalyptic vision of the future, *Riddley Walker*, (that is, the tapestry depicting the legend of St Eustace), *Blue Poles* engulfs us all in its impenetrable veils and mysteries. In a culture of counterfeit images, the direct perception of a work such as *Blue Poles* produces a devastating effect of cultural inferiority in the viewer. The following passage from *Riddley Walker* might even be the literal response of local artists (certainly the accent is right) when confronted by the enormity of this cultural gap:

Now you're talking jus like me I don't know how many times I've said that. Now you see the woal think what I'm getting at its why I'm always strest and straint I'm just a woar out man. Riddley we aint as good as them befor us. Weve come way way down from what they ben time back way back. May be it wer the barms what done it poysening the lan or when they made a hoal in what they callit the O Zoan.[4]

The problem with *Blue Poles* is of course that it is concrete proof of our provincialism. It is one of the few art objects of indisputable quality and presence that can be apprehended directly here in Australia. In a sense, it undermines the second-hand reality of the mechanically reproduced image which otherwise saturates our consciousness, determining our view of ourselves and of the external world.

As Terry Smith pointed out ten years ago, provincialism appears primarily as 'an attitude of subservience to an externally imposed hierarchy of cultural values'.[5] But most of us treat such a projection as if it were a construction of reality, when in fact it is a culturally relative viewpoint. The patterns of provincialism are deeply etched in Australia.

Typically, relentless provincialism is marked by the tensions between two antithetical positions: a defiant urge to localism (a claim for the possibility and validity of 'making good original art right here'); and a reluctant recognition that the generative innovations in art, and the criteria for standards of 'quality', 'originality', 'interest', 'forcefulness' etc., are determined externally. But far from encouraging 'innocent art of naive purity, untainted by too much thinking', provincialism in fact produces highly self-conscious art 'obsessed with the problem of what its identity ought to be.'[6]

Waves of hope that the provincial bind can be broken recur

cyclically in Australian art. In the 1920s 'nativeness' was celebrated. In the late 1940s a number of painters (later called the 'Antipodeans') placed their faith in a localism pursued with a sharp awareness of European traditions. During the 1950s and 1960s, following the influence of Abstract Expressionism, hope grew for the possibility of an avant-garde breakthrough. In 1974, in the 'inventiveness encouraged by open form sculpture, process, environmental and performance art', and during the late 1970s and early 1980s, the provincial bind was evident in the attempt by some artists and curators to blend the exoticism of Aboriginal culture with certain manifestations of contemporary art.[7] This artificial blending culminated in the French curator Suzanne Pagé's exhibition *From Another Continent: the Dream and the Real* (1983) at ARC Musée d'Art Moderne de la Ville de Paris.[8]

Today, in 1984, we place our hope in what the English critic John Roberts has termed 'the re-emergence of a strong urban-based art, orientated towards mimicry and destruction of the codes and signs of consumerism'.[9] These sentiments invite us to exaggerate our natural tendencies towards mimicry, to emphasise rather than hide our provincialism, even to bathe ostentatiously in it. For once the call from the other side of the world is congruent with our real cultural condition. It seems that at some moment each succeeding generation of artists in Australia expresses the sentiment 'Australia is now part of the art scene', only later to recognise their hopeless invisibility and powerlessness.[10] By employing strategies of mimicry, deconstruction and even hyper-conformism, 'invisibility' and 'powerlessness' can now be turned to our advantage.[11] With this realisation we are also witnessing an inversion of the normal patterns of art production in Australia, rooted as they are in low self-esteem. The shift is from the hitherto pervasive condition of 'anorexia nervosa' (small, tentative, self-effacing and ultimately self-destructive outputs) to a condition resembling 'bulimia' (binge-eating and vomiting). In the latter case, we see this in an over-excessive consumption of images and their regurgitation in a manner which is psychologically motivated and completely (often defiantly) unrelated to those market forces (the proverbial 'hunger for pictures') which seem to have stimulated art production in Europe and America.

The wide-ranging image consumption and regurgitation results not in the death of the author but in his or her apparent fragmentation. Wolfgang Max Faust has called this process the 'wilful dissociation of subjectiveness and style'. The image has become the site of a transient fascination that represents not the unity of the one ego but a multiple subjective view. Each painting becomes a battleground, an arena of conflict where 'the artist's visions and longings face a showdown with his or her knowledge of art history. A momentary irritation caused by some picture from a magazine or television ad, an art book or a dream, battles with the need to make an image that is authentically of and about the self.'[12]

Dick Watkins is in many ways the pioneer of this tendency in Australia and he has for some time been engaged in the digestion and regurgitation of Pablo Picasso and Jackson Pollock. Recently he came up with another Pollock that he ominously entitled *City of the Living Dead plus Zombie Holocaust* (1982–3).[13] This title reminds us that when there is no room left in hell, the dead will rise up and walk the earth. In other words, when authority ceases to be representative beware the dispossessed lest they rise up in revolt against everything held sacred to the prevailing order and inherit the ruins of a shattered ideology.[14] In *Riddley Walker* it is only the dispossessed who survive the nuclear holocaust and, by virtue of their survival, it is their interpretation of the remaining fragments of civilisation (no matter how pathetically misconstrued) on which the new culture is built. Cultural meaning is reforged by the bricoleurs of the post-industrial, post-nuclear age. As George Miller's popular films, *Mad Max* and *Mad Max II (The Road Warrior)* seem to suggest, Australia is already the landscape of the future and it is no coincidence that the degenerated language in *Riddley Walker* echoes the all too familiar strains of the Australian accent. In this land of the living dead our 'strategies of mimicry' are no more than adaptions of primitive principles of magic, particularly the Law of Similarity whereby the magician implies that he can produce any effect he desires by merely imitating it.[15] Some Aboriginal folklore already confirms Australia as the land of the dead: 'If the spirits stray from their path to their totemic country or island of the dead, the white cockatoos alone will see them and give a piercing cry of warning. Their cry screams out across Arnhem Land today as they continue to warn the living of the presence of the spirits in the bush.'[16]

The recent and brutal history of Australia is strewn with many corpses. For example the term 'isles of the dead' referred to those islands off the western coast of Australia where Aboriginal tribes, often sick and dying from their lack of resistance to the most harmless of white man's diseases, were herded together with no regard for their totemic differences and left to die. Another island, Tasmania, is the infamous site of a near genocide.[17]

This social history is of course a metaphor for our cultural present. While the dot-screen of mechanical reproduction renders all images equivalent, interchangeable, scale-less and surface-less, the consumption and regurgitation or 're-creation' of these images reinvests them with an aura, surface, substance and scale entirely different from their corresponding 'originals'. In this sense mechanical reproduction is a purgatory or limbo for image patterns. Like disembodied souls floating textureless in books, they are waiting to be reborn, to be recreated, to feel the actuality of their reality. The mechanical reproduction of images is a form of death (crucifixion) – when resurrected onto new surfaces these images remain 'stigmatised' by the marks of their death.[18] Thus 're-created', paintings often appear unnaturally monochrome, faded like poor xeroxes, 'out-of-register', excessively grainy, or carry residual traces of a dot-screen.

The possibilities of painting in Australia in 1984 allow the collision of several image patterns onto one surface – 'worlds in collision' where the worlds might be 'xerox satellites'. In this sense our culture is an Island of the Dead and our paintings facilitate the Return of the Living Dead. As our work too passes into reproduction, we realise that our painting, like our cultural condition, is destined to be a kind of 'perpetual mourning'.

I never sung no beginning because you wont never fynd no beginning its long gone and far pas. What ever youre after yowl never fynd the beginning of it thats why yowl all ways be too late. Onlyes thing youwl ever fynd is the end of things. What ever happens itwl be what you dint want to happen. What ever dont happen thatwl be the thing you wantit. Take your choosing how like youwl get what you dont wont.[19]

Notes

1 Giancarlo Politi and Helena Kontova, 'Interview with Enzo Cucchi', *Flash Art* (November 1983) p. 20.

2 Ibid., p. 16.

3 Papunya is the Aboriginal settlement where a now flourishing Aboriginal art movement in Western materials began in the early 1970s.

4 Russell Hoban, *Riddley Walker* (London: Picador 1982), p. 120.

5 Terry Smith, 'The Provincialism Problem', *Artforum* (September 1974), p. 54.

6 Robert Hughes, *The Art of Australia*, rev. ed. (England: Harmondsworth, 1970), p. 134.

7 Terry Smith, op. cit., p. 57; for a discussion of the drawbacks of this attitude, see my essay 'Locality Fails' in this collection.

8 See Jill Montgomery, 'Australia – The French Discovery of 1983', *Art & Text*, no. 12 & 13, (1983–4).

9 John Roberts, 'Principles of Motion', *Art Monthly*, (February 1984), p. 17.

10 For example, see Royston Harpur, 'An Important Academy', *The Field* (National Gallery of Victoria catalogue, 1968), p. 92.

11 See John Young and Terry Blake 'On Some Alternatives to the Code in the Age of Hyperreality: The Hermit and the City-Dweller', *Art & Text*, no. 2 (winter 1981), p. 7.

12 Woflgang Max Faust, '"Du hast keine Chance. Nutze sie!" With it and against it: Tendencies in Recent German Art', *Artforum* (September 1981), p. 39.

13 Exhibited at Pinacotheca, Melbourne and Yuill Crowley, Sydney in 1983.

14 Glyn Banks, 'Mulheimer Freiheit: The Return of the Living Dead', *Art Monthly*, (February 1984).

15 J.G. Frazer, *The Golden Bough* (Macmillan 1970), p. 14.

16 Jennifer Isaacs ed., *Australian Dreaming – 40,000 years of Aboriginal History* (Lansdowne Press 1980), p. 229.

17 Daisy Bates, *Passing of the Aborigines* (London: Butler and Tanner, 1938), p. 93.

18 Some artists, recognising this, have begun to make paintings which attempt to defy mechanical reproduction: for example, Sigmar Polke's *Heroes in the Air*, *Artforum*, December 1983, pp. 52–53.

19 Hoban, op. cit., p. 147.

First published in ZG/Art & Text *(joint issue), New York, July 1984.*

Imants Tillers as a Site of Conflict
1990

In a memorial address at the Wollongong City Gallery, New South Wales, in 1988, Imants Tillers spoke of the turmoil in his ancestral homeland Latvia, and the way this and other issues are manifested in his work.

I feel very honoured to be asked to give the second Bob Sredersas Memorial Lecture, following in the distinguished footsteps of Daniel Thomas who gave the first lecture last year.

As some of you may already know, Bob Sredersas arrived in Wollongong from Lithuania in 1950 and worked at the steelworks until his retirement. His personal passion, however, was to collect works of art, and on a meagre labourer's salary he managed to amass a collection which is today valued at one million dollars. Before he died in 1982 he donated this collection to the City of Wollongong and it forms the basis of the collection of the Wollongong City Art Gallery. Bob's motivation was not status or financial reward, but obviously a passion for art. To quote Nina Oliver, who visited his fibro home in the 1960s:

> Every wall was covered with paintings, from ceiling to floor, even the kitchen. They were wonderful paintings, propped up behind the stove, on a shelf above the toilet, under the bed. The furniture was sparse – a table and wooden chairs, linoleum on the floor. But you couldn't see the walls; there was no space between the paintings.

There are many things familiar to me about Bronius ('call me Bob') Sredersas, even though I never met him – for my parents too came as 'DPs' (displaced persons) from the Baltic after the Second World War. They came from Latvia, a sister country to Lithuania and, like Bob, arrived in Australia alone and penniless but grateful after the tribulations of wartime to start a new and better life. Having married in a German camp, my father Imants ('call me Harry'), like Bob, began work here as a labourer for the Water Board at Woronora, and my mother worked as a live-in domestic help for nearly two years. These experiences are common to many immigrants who arrived here in the late 1940s. It is partly for this reason that I wanted to give this lecture.

I had two titles for this talk. Firstly I wanted to call it 'Imants Tillers as a Site of Conflict', and then it occurred to me that what I wanted to say could be described equally well as 'On Incommensurability and the Realm of Possibility'. Now I think it could even be called 'I am Latvian'.

The year 1988 has been remarkable. In Australia we have witnessed Aboriginal people, descendants of the victims of the first European settlement in 1788, not boycott the bicentennial celebrations, but actively use them as an opportunity to publicise their grievances and causes as well as their cultural heritage. Certainly Aboriginal art and culture has had wider circulation and visibility this year than ever before.

However, the Aboriginal presence in what might have been a year of mourning for them is not what I wanted to talk about, but about the homeland of my parents and of Bob Sredersas – the Baltic countries – for it is here that an equally remarkable thing is taking place.

In 1982 I wrote an essay entitled 'Locality Fails' in which I suggested an unexpected connectedness could exist between events in places remote from each other, and that this connectedness could allow an experimenter (an artist) in one place to affect the state of a system in another remote (apparently unconnected) place. Ironically, this principle has come to haunt me in 1988. For how else can we explain the changes in Riga, Vilnius and Tallinn in our bicentennial year?

When the Soviet Union, in recognition of the resurgent nationalism in the Baltic republics, gave official status to the flags which Latvia and Lithuania flew as independent countries but which had been outlawed for nearly fifty years, there were incredible scenes reported even on Australian television and in the printed media. When did these distant regions last make international news? The parliaments of Latvia and Lithuania also voted to give official status to their own languages, replacing Russian, in far-reaching moves that sought to redeem President Gorbachev's pledge for the devolution of political power. In Riga, the Latvian capital, more than 150,000 people turned out when the old maroon and white flag of independent Latvia was unfurled at an emotional rally in a park on the city's outskirts.

In Vilnius, the Lithuanian capital, an estimated 100,000 people took part in city-wide processions leading to Gediminas Tower on the city's main square, where the yellow, green and red flag of independent Lithuania flew for the first time since 1940.

While one could say that these are small concessions and that the Soviet leadership has no intention of relinquishing political power, nevertheless these changes have provoked intense emotions. In Latvia, the issue of national identity is particularly sensitive because, unlike in either Estonia or Lithuania, the indigenous population has become a minority.

When I was asked to do a special project for the bicentenary issue of *Art and Australia* I wanted to address the issue of identity and power relations in the Baltic rather than in Australia. But this was in March before the dramatic changes that I have described began to be reported in the media. My work was a gatefold based on my painting *Words of Wisdom*. The painting consisted simply of a bald typewritten text on an abstract but evocative background. The words were a paraphrase of a poem by Latvian poet Zinaīda Lazda:

> In this land by the River Daugava and by the sea we are to live out our days in sorrow and in joy. With hatred we will answer the enemy who comes to humble and to plunder our native land.

But I am no partisan or Latvian-in-exile. I have an ambiguous and ambivalent relationship to the homeland of my parents and its cultural heritage. I was born in Australia and have no doubts that I am Australian. However, when I first went to school I could not speak any English, only Latvian. Now, I have the vocabulary in Latvian of a three-year-old child. In part this loss of my native tongue has been due to a natural atrophy through lack of use, but I now feel that it was also in part due to a youthful rebellion against the enormous responsibility of keeping a dying culture alive on the other side of the globe.

When I made my first trip to Latvia with my Australian wife it was from Paris in 1976. There, just before leaving, we saw a film by one of the fathers of avant-garde film in the USA, Jonas Mekas. Mekas was born in Lithuania and he arrived in the USA as a displaced person. His film was called *Reminiscences of a Journey to Lithuania*. It was a very moving account of his experiences of going back and being reunited with the relations and friends he had left behind, as well as all the facets of daily life there – so different to his new life in New York. My response to going to Latvia, a country I thought I was already familiar with even though I had never been there before, was in a sense prefigured and intensified by Mekas's film.

I now have vivid memories of visiting the ramshackle farmhouse at Salaspils (an area that was out of bounds to tourists) where my father grew up, virtually next door to the site of a former Nazi concentration camp. In its place now stood a desolate monument to those who had died there. There is also the intense memory of drinking cold, fermented birch sap with the family of my mother's childhood friend Astra at their country vegetable plot.

In Latvia I was a kind of de facto visitor, a surrogate for my parents, visiting their old haunts and their now aged relatives and friends. The other side to this was a feeling of detachment and the sense that the 'memories' of Latvia I had before I went there, of beautiful lakes and forests, were but phantoms – not based on lived experience at all. Latvia of course was now a modern country, though impoverished by our standards and not the nineteenth-century rural paradise I had half expected. Also, there was a pervasive, underlying anxiety with all our hosts – the need to be careful about what was said and where one went. One felt under surveillance all the time and there were constant signs wherever one went that this was an occupied country.

My own experiences and Mekas's great film alerted me to the possibility of working within an avant-garde tradition and yet being able to express at the same time a powerful emotional and spiritual content.

Slides from that trip subsequently became part of a work that I completed in 1978: *Reminiscences of a Journey to Latvia*. In 1985 I used the title of another of Jonas Mekas's films *Lost Lost Lost*. Mekas's film records the confusion, bewilderment, relief and dislocation of the crowds of Balts and other refugees at the moment of their arrival in the ports of New York. My parents, too, could have been caught in that film, for they had wanted to go to America – but circumstances, change, or serendipity in the postwar confusion resulted in them going to Australia instead. Therefore I am Australian, not American. Such is the fragility of national identity.

While there are many competing themes and motifs in my work, I thought that for this lecture it would be appropriate to touch on how my particular ethnic origins might have manifested themselves in my work. There are six ways in which this might be discerned:

1. The use of foreign languages in my work, particularly words and phrases in languages that I don't speak or understand, the meaning of which is accessible in translation. This could be a sign of alienation, displacement or loss. A reminder perhaps of the loss of language, of heritage, or homeland – like the loss of part of oneself.

2. Addressing issues of power. Of centres and satellites. To be Latvian has meant, historically, being dominated by powerful neighbours – powerful in the economic, political, military and cultural sense. In Sigmar Polke's formulation of this, *Higher Beings Command – Paint the Upper Right Corner Black!* And we obey.

There is a limit to what art can do in the real world – I make no pretence to changing the inequities of the world – but at least in my work I like sometimes to invert/subvert/pervert the existing power relations within the art world to accommodate the cultural priorities of a minority – myself. Speed, flexibility of response and adaptability are virtues in this situation even if it is only ultimately in order to obey.

3. Sometimes there is an allusion to hidden content – a secret: like the historical aspirations of Latvians for nationhood and independence. In the late nineteenth and early twentieth century it was essential for such aspirations to remain secret or encoded. This has again been necessary in Latvia since 1940 with the forced incorporation of Latvia into the Soviet Union and the ruthless Russianisation that has been taking place ever since.

In my work this has been manifested in the idea of invisible layers in certain paintings, for example in the ASSISI series. The final visible layer often has an essential relationship to what was painted over – to what is now hidden and known only to me. In some paintings there is an allusion to a Latvian iconography that might only be interpreted as such by Latvians. Generally speaking, these Baselitz wanderers might easily be seen as figures from Latvian rustic life or as heroes of Latvian folklore. The use of canvasboards themselves, slightly shonky, *hokey* materials from which to construct epically scaled works, might parallel the grandiose pretensions of an essentially rural country of former serfs and peasants.

4. Use of imagery 'borrowed' from Latvian book illustrations and other sources. These images would be easily recognised by Latvians and would seem 'ethnic' to non-Latvians. This is a way of

perpetuating Latvian elements alongside more powerful elements within an Australian and international context. Iwona Blazwick, the curator of my exhibition at the Institute of Contemporary Art in London, described how the nineteenth- and twentieth-century masterworks I had repainted had often been invaded by fragments of 'native' culture. I would add that these fragments could be 'Antipodean', Aboriginal or Baltic.

5. The idea of proliferation. Since I started to work on composite paintings made of canvasboard panels in 1981, I have been counting them: I am now up to 19,301. This is commemorated in the painting *19301 + as of October.* It is also the title of my forthcoming exhibition at the National Art Gallery in Wellington early next year. Elsewhere I have compared my work to a huge all-encompassing book, where each canvasboard panel is a page. As the French poet Mallarmé wrote in 1895: 'Everything, in the world, exists to end up in a book.' The panels have been numbered right from the start and the panel count is continuous from 1 to ∞. All modes of art can be accommodated within this book, and all modes of expression: from the trivial to the serious, the banal to the profound, the pious to the blasphemous, et cetera. As I have stated elsewhere, my intention is the exhaustion of all possible categories, and if I cannot finish this task I will assign someone else to continue it.

With this idea of proliferation and the power that comes from picturing or mapping one's psychic terrain there is a strong correspondence with the stockpile of Latvian folksongs which, in the absence of more developed and sophisticated cultural institutions, served as oral repositories of the Latvian cultural heritage. Since they began to be collected and recorded it has been estimated that there are millions of different songs – almost a different one for every Latvian living today. These folksongs describe every facet of the environment, recording the daily life of the Latvian people. At the folkloric festival in Latvia earlier this year Jānis Peters wrote in the programme notes:

On the dawn of the twentieth century Latvia was born. And the world noticed it. Because Latvia was a child of sorrow. Sorrow, because our country Latvia, our republic Latvia was born in great pains. We have dreamt and ached for our country. We have cherished and fought for it. We have defended it and we still do.

Central to this defence is the folksong:

Latvians believe in their ancient folklore which has saved the nation from destruction. The folksong to which we have given a short and euphonic name – DAINA – has strengthened our people in political as well as culturally historical feuds.

It is also interesting for me to compare, though they are in some ways incomparable, these folksongs as the bearers of cultural meaning to the Aboriginal Dreamings. As Robert Hughes puts it, the Dreamings are the world's spirit ancestors; they brought the world out of chaos, formed it and filled it with plants, insects, animals and fish, and created human society. They exist in vast numbers, and there is one for every nameable entity.

To me, the process of appropriation of other works of art and their incorporation into my ever-expanding Book of Power is also a process of naming, like that of the Aboriginal Dreamings and the

Latvian DAINAs, except that my chosen world is the world of art.

6. The title of my lecture was 'Imants Tillers as a Site of Conflict' and I do not seem to have addressed this topic directly at all. Here I was thinking of the fragmentation of the self in a process that has been described as the 'wilful dissociation of subjectiveness and style', where the image becomes the site of a transient fascination that represents not the unity of one ego but a multiple subjective view. Each painting becomes a battleground where 'the artist's visions and longings face a showdown with his or her knowledge of art history. Thus a momentary irritation caused by some picture from a magazine or television ad, art book or a dream battles with the need to make an image that is authentically of and about the self.'[1]

For some time I have believed that this was happening in my paintings too. That they were a battleground. The blank canvasboards were waiting to be filled and the images of other artists were waiting to fill them. I was the referee, the adjudicator. The potential images would battle it out with each other for supremacy. Sometimes Kiefer or Baselitz would triumph: at other times it would be de Chirico or Sherrie Levine or Colin McCahon or Michael Nelson Jagamara. I alone would determine the fate of their images – they could become thirty feet long or minuscule – executed hastily or with great love and precision. Latvia, of course, has always been a battleground and its people resilient and resistant enough to keep their identity intact despite the odds.

7. The idea of incommensurability. My process is not always like a battleground. The all-inclusive potential of my project – as the accumulation of canvasboard panels inches its way to infinity – allows for the idea of incommensurability. At times there is no

attempt by me to transform, assimilate or synthesise these streams into a more homogeneous entity but rather they simply exist side by side with each other. They are not measurable in terms of each other and the only similarity may be that they all consist of the same canvasboard particles.

For me this sense of incommensurability is a model of tolerance – of the accommodation of differences where elements do not have to justify themselves to each other or subordinate themselves to a larger, more important schema. This is the only way a small but ancient culture like Latvia can survive – if there is room for incommensurable differences in the larger scheme of things. Perhaps it is the only way that the remnants of Aboriginal culture can survive too. This is in the realm of possibility.

Notes

1 Woflgang Max Faust, '"Du hast keine Chance. Nutze sie!" With it and against it: Tendencies in Recent German Art', *Artforum* (September 1981), p. 39.

Edited transcript of the second Bob Sredersas Memorial Lecture delivered at the Wollongong City Gallery, 17 November 1988. First published in Art and Australia, *volume 27, number 3, Autumn 1990, 422–29.*

Perturbations in the Image Field
1996

'Postcolonialism', 'globalisation', 'the global network' – these are rapidly becoming the new catchphrases of the 1990s. The Italian art magazine *Flash Art*, always quick to respond to fashion, now puts on its cover an image which it supposes to engage the concept of 'Global Art'. Also in Australia, we recently witnessed the arrival of a new magazine, provocatively entitled *World Art*. We all know that headquarters is no longer Paris or New York, but how can it be Melbourne where *World Art* is now published? What if similar publishing enterprises are under way in a number of other equally peripheral cities? In the opening up of this vast new image field we cannot assume that the new players want necessarily to be passive, compliant, democratic or well-behaved. I don't want to suggest for a moment, that the art world would necessarily follow the same trajectory as some recent post-communist social trends, notably the growth of a global mafia with the most feared criminal elements now being those originating from the former Soviet Union. However, the new groups or individuals who suddenly become visible may want to take centre stage, whether their launch pad is Melbourne, St Petersburg, Papunya or Auckland, and hijack the discourses. In Australia, for example, we have seen the unexpected, meteoric rise of Aboriginal art which in the last three to four years has totally eclipsed the work of white contemporary Australian artists, not only in the international arena, but at home too. Aboriginal art in its myriad forms must now be considered mainstream Australian art – a most unlikely scenario even ten years ago.

Colonised, marginalised, peripheral cultures feel angry, dispossessed, and given changed circumstances can be out for revenge: the proverbial Revolt of the Margins. I am quite familiar with the situation in Latvia for example, whose small population of indigenous people have been colonised for at least 700 years, yet through an extremely resistant character have managed to keep their language and aspects of their ancient oral culture intact. It is fascinating to discover that the Baltic Germans who were the rulers in this area of the Baltic from the thirteenth century following its conquest by the Teutonic Knights, regarded the area as 'wilderness'. Indeed Baltic German authors sometimes used the expression *das Unland* to describe the region. This term in a sense suggests that not merely were the pagan inhabitants less than fully human, but the land was not really the land; it only became 'land' in the full sense when developed by the Christian Germans. The parallels with colonial Australia and the British concept of *terra nullius* are striking.

Then there is the issue of the coloniser's language and the control exerted through the naming and renaming of places. In James Breslin's recent biography of the American artist Mark Rothko, I noted that his birthplace Dvinsk in Russia is actually the Russian name for the Latvian town of Daugavpils on the River Daugava, and that when he left for America he sailed from the port of Libau, the Russian name for my mother's birthplace Liepāja. Evidently Rothko's childhood memories of this Latvian part of Russia, which is what it was in the early twentieth century, was something he often referred to. Breslin makes the point that the diffused light in this northern part of the world is something that inhabits Rothko's abstract paintings. 'The Latvian painter has a special love for diffused outdoor light which seems to penetrate the bodies and emanate from them...a light that reappears within Rothko's paintings, an illumination glimpsed through a hazy doorway or window, a light longed for but beyond reach.' In our postcolonial world we can find this light also in the work of another Latvian-born artist, Vija Celmins, currently the subject of a major retrospective in the United States.

'Postcolonialism' carries strong and valid emotions associated with past historic injustices, often with subtleties and complexities which easily evade outsiders. We should not assume that the artists who engage with the colonial histories of their own countries will necessarily be thankful or respectful of the forces within the art world which promote their visibility. As the Latvian poet Zinaida Lazda once put it: 'in this land by the River Daugava and by the sea we are to live out our days in sorrow and joy. With hatred we will answer the enemy who comes to humble and to plunder our native land.'

Multiply this valid sentiment by all the small countries and distinct ethnic groups emerging from a colonised past and we have a formula for large-scale chaos. But on the other hand the artists from these countries have a ready-made and often profound content to their work and an urgency to express it which is often lacking in the West. As Norbert Weber, the artistic director of the Baltic Sea Biennale in 1992 at the Rostock Kunsthalle puts it:

> For the first Biennale to be held in Rostock after the great political upheavals in Eastern Europe this open-mindedness was not only an obligation but represented a true chance. Our confrontation with a truth that transcended mere aesthetic presence made the issues of the Western art market seem comparatively secondary. In view of the timeless yearning for happiness (for example) reflected in the faces

of the children in Valts Kleins' photographs, every attempt to present only the latest innovations of a hyped-up scene appeared absurdly beside the point. Our eyes were opened for a meaningful involvement with the content of art.

I might add that this situation also applies within Australia to the Aboriginal people, who are only now beginning to emerge successfully from a colonial past of two hundred years – thus the work of an artist like Gordon Bennett has particular poignancy for us at this moment. But add together all these new artists and their specific cultural and historical contexts and one can see that the new visible global cultural environment is one of unprecedented complexity – one which could be characterised as a 'turbulent field'.

Fred Emery in his book *Systems Thinking* explains that the dynamic properties of turbulent fields arise not simply from the interaction of identifiable component systems but from the field itself. Turbulence results from the complexity and multiple characters of the interconnections. Individual organisations (or individuals) cannot adapt successfully simply through their direct interactions since they cannot predict the size or consequence of the actions they set into train. We could certainly view the new global situation (since the fall of communism) politically and socially as a turbulent one. This situation seems to be echoed in the art world. In addition, one of the factors pertinent to the new global art world I am particularly aware of (since I draw on the vast mass of printed images in circulation for my work), is that the radical increase in speed, scope and capacity for communication results in a quantity of information received at such a rate that it can scarcely be processed, not to speak of making decisions on its basis. As more and more artists plug themselves into a global framework (and there are increasingly more and more artists), this will be the causal environment in which they will also find themselves.

Since the early 1970s, however, there has been a scientific revolution in our midst – chaos theory. It is a science which relates neither to the very large (as does the theory of relativity) nor to the very small (quantum mechanics) but to events and processes at our human scale. Chaos theory in fact comes out of the study of turbulence and the behaviour of complex natural systems such as the weather. One of the first and most amazing discoveries of chaos theory is the so-called butterfly effect – the notion that tiny differences in the input into a complex system can produce overwhelming differences in output – which embodies the rather poetic notion that a butterfly fluttering its wings today in Beijing can transform storm systems next month in New York. The butterfly effect has acquired a more technical name: sensitive dependence on initial conditions. This principle also seems to apply to all sorts of other phenomena including cultural phenomena.

As a cultural theory, chaos theory certainly empowers marginal and peripheral artists and introduces some instability into the rational and tyrannical logic of provincialism – the hitherto persuasive argument that the cultural peripheries are powerless to resist the agendas and hierarchies of the cultural centres. Through a twist of fate, a chain of events, a magnification of effects, they could be determining the agendas of those so-called centres.

Chaos theory might also have application at the more specific level of an artist's oeuvre. One might recall the German critic Wolfgang Max Faust's writings in 1981 referring to the neo-expressionist works of artists like Dokoupil, Dahn or Kippenberger:

wide ranging image consumption and regurgitation results not in the death of the author but his or her fragmentation – the wilful dissociation of subjectiveness and style – the image has become the site of a transient fascination that represents not the unity of one ego but a multiple subjective view. Each painting becomes a battleground, an arena of conflict where the artist's visions and longings face a showdown with his or her knowledge of art history. A momentary irritation caused by some picture from a magazine or television ad, or an art book or a dream battles with a need to make an image that is authentically of and about the self.

In hindsight, after chaos theory, one could reinterpret this relationship of the artist to his or her sources and to his or her artistic productions as a complex system which is being pushed to the edges of chaos by the turbulence of the surrounding image field. In the early 1990s we could argue that the image field has become even more turbulent.

Ilya Prigogine (a Nobel Prize Winner in 1977 for Chemistry) and Isabelle Stengers have made further advances in this fertile area of scientific theory in their book *Order Out of Chaos*. The book contains some incredible insights and bizarre propositions which seem to have relevant implications for the new global art world in which we now find ourselves. In this paper it is only possible to touch very briefly and superficially on some of them but I recommend this book to everyone. Their ideas are certainly beginning to seep through into many other disciplines beyond their field of chemistry – the most recent example being a reformulation of Darwinian evolution in the light of their approach. The key idea in *Order Out of Chaos* is that in 'far from equilibrium conditions' (i.e. at the edge of chaos) not only can small inputs yield huge startling effects (the so-called butterfly effect) but the entire system may suddenly and spontaneously reorganise itself in ways that strike us as bizarre. The argument is based on observations of certain chemical phenomena and the implication is that somehow matter is active rather than passive. In Prigoginian terms, all systems contain subsystems which are continually 'fluctuating' and at times a single fluctuation or combination of them may become so powerful, as a result of positive feedback, that it shatters the pre-existing organisation. At this revolutionary moment – Prigogine calls it a 'singular moment' or a 'bifurcation' point – it is inherently impossible to determine in advance which direction change will take – whether the system will disintegrate into 'chaos' or leap to a new higher and more differentiated level of 'order' or 'organisation', which they call a 'dissipative structure'. According to Prigogine and Stengers it is the processes associated with randomness and openness that lead to higher levels of organisation, such as dissipative structures. Chance indeed nudges what remains of the system down a new path of development and once that path is chosen (from among many) determinism takes over until the next bifurcation point is reached.

According to Alvin Toffler in his foreword to their book, 'by offering rigorous ways of modelling qualitative change, Prigogine and Stengers shed light on the concept of revolution. By explaining how successive instabilities give rise to transformatory change, they illuminate organisation theory. They throw light also on certain psychological processes: for example "innovation" which the authors see as associated with "non-average" behaviour of the kind that arises under non-equilibrium conditions.'

The 'spontaneous self-organisation of non-equilibrium systems' which Prigogine and Stengers propose has some fascinating spin-offs. For example, at the moment that this spontaneous self-organisation occurs – say within a chemical reaction – the molecules seem to be able to communicate with each other directly to achieve a coherent, synchronised change. Locality fails. At this critical moment the individual constituent particles seem innately to comprehend their unique position-to-be within the larger but as-yet-unformed whole.

As we have seen, when there are perturbations or fluctuations in a non-equilibrium system close to chaos, at the bifurcation points, things are unpredictable – they can go either way. In hindsight the demise of the Soviet Union seems inevitable and it has been treated that way even though before its collapse absolutely no one predicted it. From Prigogine we know that at the bifurcation point the outcome is impossible to predict. Things could have turned out completely differently: the Berlin Wall might still be standing, the crackdown on the Baltic States in January 1990 during the Gulf War might have been successful, and the August 1991 coup against Gorbachev not even staged since it would have been unnecessary. And Dvinsk would still be Dvinsk, not Daugavpils. Furthermore, I doubt whether in the art world we would be talking about 'postcolonialism' and global art.

As we know from the butterfly effect, a chain of events can have a crisis point that magnifies small changes. I think the Korean Fluxus artist Nam June Paik must have recognised this when he wrote his article on President Landsbergis of Lithuania for *Artforum* in December 1990 before the critical events had occurred. Incidentally it is interesting to think of the Fluxus movement in global terms – spanning Asia, America and Europe but also in terms of chaos theory and Prigogine – since many of the Fluxus artists were very interested in processes associated with randomness and openness. As Paik wrote: 'the East European revolution produced a playwright-president, Václav Havel in Czechoslovakia, but few people know that it also produced a Fluxus-president: Vytautas Landsbergis, the president of Lithuania. During the spring of 1990, the image of the bespectacled and stoop-shouldered "music professor" paraded across the TV news every day. He successfully defied the blockade of Soviet Power and the "benevolent" advice of the Western press to go slow lest he destroy the superpower summit. When Gorbachev received the Nobel Prize, Landsbergis sent him a congratulatory telegram: "Your Majesty".'

This audacious David-and-Goliath situation strongly reminded Paik of Landsbergis' best friend, George Maciunas – the founder of the Fluxus movement. Landsbergis and Maciunas were both the sons of well-off architects and were best friends at school in Kaunas, Lithuania, in the last peaceful days of prewar Europe. Landsbergis remained in Lithuania and Maciunas ended up in New York. Landsbergis, although still confined in Soviet Lithuania, evidently contributed musical compositions for a number of Fluxus concerts and participated several times in Fluxus mail-art events, such as those organised by Mieko Shiomi from Osaka, Japan. As part of her 'Spatial Poem No. 5', Mieko Shiomi proposed an 'Open Event': 'Open something which is closed; Please describe to me how you did it and what happened by your performance. Your reports will be recorded on the world map.' So we note on the world map in the area occupied by Lithuania, the name of Vytautas Landsbergis. And the following description: 'A day after my return from the country to my flat in Vilnius, I opened the lid of my piano and hit the keyboard of

F sharp. When the sound died down completely, I went to my study to continue on some unfinished work. Vilnius 1 p.m. July 23, 1972'.

I would like to imagine that the so-called Baltic Way on 23 August 1989, when one million Latvians, Lithuanians and Estonians joined hands in a continuous human chain across 680 kilometres stretching from Tallinn, the Estonian capital, in the north, through Latvia to Vilnius, the Lithuanian capital, in the south, was an event conceived in the Fluxus spirit. Was it the idea of an artist, a poet, an engineer or was it perhaps the idea of a president? This brave and defiant protest on the anniversary of the secret Nazi-Soviet pact of 1939, which consigned the Baltic States to fifty years of illegal rule by the Soviet Union, certainly made front-page news all over the world. Could the Baltic Way have been the crucial perturbation – the catalyst to the break-up of the Soviet Union?

I'm sure Maciunas would have thought that 'holding hands' was beautiful. Indeed he had his performers holding hands in New Marlborough, Massachusetts in 1977 (only a year before his death) when they performed his 'Untitled Marching Piece' at the Flux Snow Event. But I doubt that even he fully realised the power of Fluxus ideas or their imminent relevance to his former homeland. One million Balts 'holding hands' on 23 August 1989, and then a little over two years later, Lithuania, Estonia, Latvia are independent states and the iron grip of the Soviet Union is broken, at least for the time being.

First published in Rudi Fuchs, Paula Savage, Dorine Mignot and Wystan Curnow (eds), The World Over/Under Capricorn: Art in the Age of Globalisation, *exhibition catalogue, Wellington and Amsterdam: National Art Gallery and Stedelijk Museum, 1996*

Poetic Justice – A Case Study
(Due Allocation of Reward of Virtue and Punishment of Vice)
1994

When the organisers of the *Commitments* exhibition proposed that I collaborate with an artist of Aboriginal descent, my interest was certainly aroused.[1] I had worked collaboratively before, but never with an Aboriginal artist. Here was my chance. For some time I had been a little envious of Tim Johnson who had found a way to collaborate with a number of the Papunya artists, indeed, arguably the most important of them all – Clifford Possum Tjapaltjarri and Michael Nelson Jagamara.[2] To me this seemed the equivalent of a regional artist of modest reputation finding a way to collaborate with Joseph Beuys or Andy Warhol. How did he do it? For the *Commitments* exhibition, it would have been very exciting for me to have worked collaboratively with one of those artists that Tim had befriended, but instead I was paired with Gordon Bennett, for a number of good reasons that will soon become apparent.

In 1985 I painted *The Nine Shots*, which combined an image from the German artist Georg Baselitz's 'Ein Neuer Typ' series of the late 1960s with *Five Dreamings* (1984) by Michael Nelson Jagamara. Both the Baselitz and the Michael Nelson Jagamara had been painted on continuous lengths of canvas. *The Nine Shots*, however, was painted on ninety-one discrete, canvasboard panels, each measuring 10" by 15". These can be assembled on the wall to form a temporary painting measuring 130" by 105". When it is not attached to a wall, *The Nine Shots* reverts to its volumetric form, a small freestanding stack; a kind of sculpture. The canvasboards used in *The Nine Shots* are of the same type as the *carton* used by the Impressionists at the turn of the century. This cheap, rigid, mobile painting support was also used by some of the Papunya artists at the genesis of the movement in the early 1970s.

Some of my appropriation works have been closely based on single images. The most faithful is probably *I Am the Door* (1985), which is a version of Sigmar Polke's *Paganini* (1982). I was attracted to this particular Polke because it was like a ready-made Tillers, done by Polke. But *The Nine Shots* belongs in a different category: it is a hybrid image. The two source images are only partially quoted, and are also subjected to distortion, fragmentation and dislocation. Thus, a direct comparison with *Five Dreamings* would reveal few direct correspondences. In some way it is stretching the word 'appropriation' to describe it as such, particularly in the context of such artistic practices as those of the American postmodernists or 'appropriation artists', such as Mike Bidlo, Jeff Koons, Sherrie Levine or even David Salle. It is more like the appropriation practice of Julian Schnabel, who is better known as a 'neo-expressionist'. Nevertheless it would be fair to say that it is because of this one work that I have been drawn into the debate about the 'postmodern appropriation of Aboriginal imagery'. Without engaging in this debate here, I would like to point out several fascinating aspects of my painting *The Nine Shots* and its reception.

Firstly, *The Nine Shots* is known to the Australian public almost exclusively through reproduction. Indeed, the debate over this work – which was not shown in the 1986 Sydney Biennale although reproduced in the catalogue – precedes the one and only occasion on which it has actually been exhibited in Australia. That was in the exhibition *A Changing Relationship – Aboriginal Themes in Australian Art 1938–1988* at the S.H. Ervin Gallery, Sydney, in 1988. In reproduction, the essential fragmented, discontinuous structure of my works is lost. What the Chilean artist Eugenio Dittborn has described as 'the literal, horizontal and vertical cuts between each panel' appear to have healed.[3] Indeed the paintings look as though they have been painted on a continuous canvas in regular rectangular sections like, for example, John Young's 'Silhouette' series. But this is just a misleading effect of the painting being photographed and reproduced. According to Dittborn, it is 'this impossibility of covering their small wounds, joints and cuts with painting' which is the essential quality of my canvasboard paintings.

Then there is the fact – which demonstrates the remarkable effect of this one painting on local critical discourse – that, unlike say Tim Johnson, my engagement with Aboriginal art is only a minor aspect of my canvasboard works. There are about twenty paintings between 1983 and 1993 which quote to a greater or lesser degree from Aboriginal sources – about twelve artists – from the more than 600 works I have completed since beginning my canvasboard project in late 1981. That is less than three per cent.

A further facet is the issue of 'error' and 'misquotation'. René Daumal in his famous essay 'The Lie of the Truth' states: 'At the beginning there was error. Truth is one, but error proliferates. Man tracks it down and cuts it up into little pieces hoping to turn it into grains of truth. But the ultimate atom will always essentially be an error, a miscalculation'.[4] Thus as Rex Butler has noted, Juan Davila, in a much-quoted attack on Tim Johnson and me – 'Aboriginality: a lugubrious game?' – misquotes me. He attributes words from my article 'Locality Fails' to me when they are in fact my paraphrase of the position which I wished to contest, not support! But, as Butler notes, 'perhaps this is not merely a contingent error on Davila's part, for in a way it is the very fate of language itself, to be misquoted'.[5]

The error is particularly significant because it inspired Gordon Bennett to paint *The Nine Ricochets (fall down black fella, jump up white fella)* as a kind of answer to *The Nine Shots*, which Davila had misrepresented as 'nine postmodernist shots aimed at the death of the primitive'.[6] In Bennett's painting on canvas, completed in 1990, the shots scatter over the surface of an image taken from old book illustrations showing us the 'true history' of Australia. The dots used to bind the images are references to Bennett's Aboriginal background – he has an Aboriginal mother and an English father – though as a diasporic Aboriginal he notes, 'in just three generations (my specific) heritage has been lost to me. Dots are my bridge to Aboriginality'.[7] As Alison Carroll notes 'on top of this image Bennett actually assembles a reference to another Tillers image, *Pataphysical Man,* and on top of this a little optical puzzle "on a single canvasboard panel" which literally confounds logical image construction'.[8]

The Nine Ricochets launched Gordon Bennett's artistic career in a spectacular manner. This work was reproduced on the back cover of Bernard Smith and Terry Smith's important book *Australian Painting 1788–1990* almost before the paint was dry. Amazing for an artist who only completed his Bachelor of Arts at Queensland College of Art in 1988. *The Nine Ricochets* also won Bennett the prestigious and lucrative Möet & Chandon prize for 1990. It was included in the important *Aratjara* exhibition in Europe, was used on its poster and seems to have been the image from this exhibition most often reproduced in magazines and newspaper reviews.

One can easily see how Bennett's painting appeals to a sense of 'poetic justice' – an Aboriginal artist using postmodern methodologies and postcolonial rhetoric to hit back at an artist who, as Fiona Foley put it in 1987, 'steals from Aboriginal culture'.[9] But in fact Gordon Bennett has intervened here on behalf of Michael Nelson Jagamara. It would have been fascinating if Michael Nelson had responded to *The Nine Shots* with his own counter-work, but then Gordon Bennett would have had no job to do.

A hidden irony of *The Nine Ricochets* is that Bennett, in quoting from *Pataphysical Man*, quotes precisely that part – the figure of the boy – which is itself a quotation from a very well-known Latvian artist and writer Jānis Jaunsudrabiņš.[10] But aren't Latvians the indigenous people of a land, a land which, until very recently, and except for brief periods before World War I and World War II, had been colonised for over seven hundred years? What difference does it make to the issue at hand if I am not descended from the colonisers of Australia, but from yet another colonised and oppressed indigenous people? Dare I suggest that Gordon Bennett's motivations in targeting *The Nine Shots* might not have been totally adversarial or critical? Could there have been (even at an unconscious level) an empathic vector as well? As Gordon wrote to me in a fax on 4 August 1993:

> It is interesting to note that the specific quotation from your work *Pataphysical Man* that I chose contained an image I had kept close to me since 1983, an image that I was keeping for use in the right painting at the right time. I was very excited to find this small

gnostic symbol of a snake nailed to a cross revealed to me (in your work) during the painting process, situated precisely where I wanted it! Maybe there is something in mental telepathy after all![11]

And what of the strange case of the first Aboriginal person to receive a PhD – Dr Eve Fesl, who is the director of Melbourne's Koorie Research Centre. Dr Fesl's thesis – the culmination of twelve years of further education – examined the treatment of Koorie languages and the use of the English language to conceal the existence of a slave trade in Australia. Dr Fesl is also a linguist and speaks not only her native language, Bandjalang, but also German, and astonishingly, Latvian and a little French.[12] She probably speaks better Latvian than I do! But why Latvian?

I would like to suggest that there is more to Bennett's painting *The Nine Ricochets* than meets the eye. It is more than a simple case of 'poetic justice' – due allocation of reward of virtue and punishment of vice – and this is the key to my collaboration with him. Certainly, beyond the overt reference to my work there are other resonances that, I would suggest in many cases, would be unknowable to Bennett himself. The question is: how did they find their way into his work? For example, the axeman in Bennett's picture is uncannily similar to any of the thirty axemen which appear in my *Conversations with the Bride* (1975). The red, superimposed canvasboard panel in *The Nine Ricochets* echoes two prior works of mine. *Erased Portrait of Murray Bail* (1985) and *The Decentred Self* (1985) both employ a single superimposed, monochrome canvasboard panel. The Pollock-like drips in the ground of *The Nine Ricochets* are contemporaneous with the start of my 'Action painting' series from February 1990, and are similar to the Pollock-like drips in early canvasboard works such as *Twilight of the Idols* (1983) and *Rapture* (1984).

There is also the uncanny resemblance between Bennett's statement in the 1991 Möet & Chandon touring exhibition catalogue and my text 'POEM at 29343', which I produced to coincide with my exhibition *The Bridge of Reversible Destiny* at Yuill/Crowley Gallery in April 1990. Both texts employ the same quotation from Colin McCahon's painting *Victory Over Death 2* (1970). Each line of our respective texts begins with the words 'I AM'.

But there are other parallels as well. What are we to make of Bennett's use of a one-point perspective construction as his personal logo and trademark pictorial device? It has its 'other', its shadow-self, in several of my pre-canvasboard works and appears in a related form on page 49 of my 1981 book *Three Facts* (the source of my image is Chinese). As Rex Butler has written, appropriation never simply works in one direction, 'the process of appropriation always proceeds in two directions, is always subject to a prior appropriation that makes it possible'.[13]

Thus when it was suggested that I collaborate with Gordon Bennett for *Commitments* we were already inextricably enmeshed. Perhaps a collaboration might disentangle us? Having agreed to collaborate, there was then the problem of how to proceed. I did not know Gordon personally – nor had I even had the opportunity to meet him until long after this paper was first presented. Then, at a certain moment, while I was doing other work – and I have recorded this moment precisely because it came so vividly to me at 1.30 p.m. on 27 July 1993 – I realised that our collaboration had already occurred. Our collaboration would be a painting of the image that I was looking at, at that precise moment – a reproduction of Giorgio de Chirico's painting *Greetings of a Distant Friend* (1916). It was up to me to execute the painting on canvasboard panels in my accustomed manner, but Gordon's work was already done.

Several days later when I rang Gordon to tell him – this was our first direct contact – I suggested to him that the collaboration had already taken place by telepathy. Understandably perhaps, he was not particularly taken with my suggestion. But it was not a provocation, it was what I believe had really taken place.

His reply to me by fax on 2 August fleshed out his perhaps justifiable concerns:

Dear Imants Tillers,
I've thought about your proposal for a work based on an image received telepathically from myself. I need to know more information before I can agree to your proposal. I want to know the details of the image and your ideas concerning it. My idea of a collaborative work is one that is produced on an equal basis. Your idea just seems a little too convenient and I must say a little patronising as well. I want to know more about your telepathy idea as I am concerned about its reference to romantic ideas surrounding Aborigines (it belongs in *Crocodile Dundee*). (By the way I was driving through the central desert between Yuendumu and Papunya at 1.30 p.m. 27 July.) If we can't come to some agreement on an equal basis than I suggest we forget about the whole idea and the exhibition – the rush for the catalogue publication is not a concern and is only a fault of the organisers of this exhibition; a blank page would suit me. Your suggestion requires a tremendous amount of trust (or gullibility) on my part so please forgive me if my fears are

unfounded but the fact remains that I don't know you...
Yours sincerely, G. Bennett.

I then sent a fax to Gordon with some details of the inadvertent references his *The Nine Ricochets* made to other works of mine – as I outlined above – and also the image that I believe he had telepathically nominated for our collaboration. However, Gordon was not content with a purely telepathic role – not amenable to my idea of a collaboration where 'collaboration' can be carried out without the conscious knowledge or indeed volition of the other party. But he did want to collaborate. So he came up with an alternative idea of his own which assembled several elements into the form of an installation. These included the faxed correspondence between us which documented the involved process of negotiation in which we had both participated, a shadow version on canvasboards of the image I had faxed to him and a stack of blank canvasboard panels – a bold act of appropriation.

For my part I went ahead with the image which I believed had been transmitted to me by Gordon – or had I, like Sigmar Polke, been commanded by higher beings? – albeit with some minor additions and alterations. And I called it, rather stubbornly: *Painting for Closed Eyes – an Experiment in Thought Transference From an Image Received Telepathically From Gordon Bennett at 1.30 p.m. on July 27, 1993.*

Notes

1 The *Commitments* exhibition presented 'works by artists from Aboriginal and non-Aboriginal backgrounds who have worked collaboratively to create artworks, to break down/through existing boundaries to create new frames of reference'. It was curated by Marshall Bell, Henrietta Fourmile, Marcia Langton and Nicholas Tsoutas and organised by the Institute of Modern Art. The exhibition was shown at the Institute of Modern Art, Brisbane, 9 September–2 October 1993; University of Southern Queensland, 15 October–5 November 1993; Artspace, Sydney, 15 April–28 May 1994; and the Canberra School of Art Gallery, 10 June–2 July 1994.

2 Contrary to popular opinion, this was not the first image I had 'appropriated' from an Aboriginal artist. The first was an untitled painting by Kaapa Mbitjana Tjampitjinpa, which had been reproduced in the 1983 book *Papunya: Aboriginal Painting From the Central Desert*. It is possible to detect traces of this image in the underlayer of my second canvasboard painting *Spirit of Place* (1983).

3 Eugenio Dittborn, 'Du carton des impressionistes: Notes for a Small Genealogy of the Canvasboard in the Pictorial Work of Imants Tillers', *Imants Tillers: Jump* (Sydney: Sherman Galleries Goodhope, 1994).

4 René Daumal, *The Lie of the Truth* (Madras and New York: Hanuman Books, 1989), p. 7.

5 Juan Davila 'Aboriginality: a Lugubrious Game?' *Art & Text,* 23–24 (March–May 1987), p. 54; Imants Tillers 'Locality Fails' *Art & Text,* 6, (winter 1982) p. 51; Rex Butler 'Two Readings of Gordon Bennett's *The Nine Ricochets*' *Eyeline* (winter/spring, 1992, p. 22.

6 Davila, p. 55.

7 Bob Lingard, 'Interview with Gordon Bennett', *Tension 17* (1989), p. 39.

8 Alison Carroll 'Gordon Bennett' Möet & Chandon touring exhibition catalogue 1991 (Möet & Chandon Australian Art Foundation, Melbourne, 1991), p. 9.

9 Quoted in Eric Michaels 'Postmodernism: a Consideration of the Appropriation of Aboriginal Imagery' Forum Papers (Institute of Modern Art, Brisbane 1989), p. 26.

10 As a diasporic Latvian it was natural for me to quote such a source. Furthermore, for a Latvian it would be instantly recognisable as a Jaunsudrabiņš rather than a Tillers.

11 I actually made a copy of this gnostic symbol – from p. 400 of Carl Jung's *Psychology and Alchemy* – in 1982 as part of a series of works called 'Suppressed Imagery'. This pencil on canvasboard panel was then recycled in December 1983 as part of the underlayer for *Pataphysical Man*.

12 Reported in the Sydney *Daily Mirror* newspaper in 1989.

13 Rex Butler, op. cit. p. 20.

This is an edited version of a paper delivered at the forum We've All Been Framed, *Artspace, Sydney, on 23 April 1994.* Midwest, *no. 5, 1994, pp. 10–15.*

Five Portraits of Murray Bail
1998

Sometime in 1985, it was decided somehow (by Murray Bail, I think) that I should paint his portrait. This was not a straightforward task as then I was anything but a portrait painter. Nevertheless over the next six years I made five valiant attempts. I started by taking photographs of my subject; sketches and even measured drawings.

I was motivated in part to repay Murray's generous flow of valuable snippets of information to me – for example that the sleepers on the Trans-Siberian railroad were made of ironbark wood from New South Wales, or that Immanuel Kant's *Critique of Pure Reason* was first published in Riga, or that German artist Anselm Kiefer's suitcase on his visit to Australia was full of expensive Cuban cigars. Murray also, when he lived near my Chippendale studio, took me one afternoon on a kind of 'Boys' Own' expedition to nearby Dangar Place, notorious scene of former NSW detective Roger Rogerson's showdown with Warren Lanfranchi. We found no bullet holes there but I came away impressed with the scope of Murray's interests. And when it came to art, Murray had impeccable taste: Douglas Huebler, Joseph Beuys, Shusaku Arakawa, Ian Fairweather, Colin McCahon, Max Beckmann, Giorgio de Chirico, Brice Marden. The small McCahon on a single 10 x 14" canvasboard panel which had pride of place in his current Elizabeth Bay flat – one of the works from the 1978 series 'Truth from the King Country – Load Bearing Structure' – is a work to covet. Luckily, Murray is also a bit of a trader so I can boast at least an Arakawa of my own, *In voice / in and around*. However, with its inscription 'to dear Margaret and Murray Bail with love!!', it still does not seem to fully belong to me.

Murray's most recent 'pearl of wisdom' for me was a photocopy of Mondrian's unlikely abstraction of an Australian gum tree, *Eucalyptus* (1912). As Murray notes, it is 'hard to tell if it's a Lemon-scented or a Ghost Gum'.

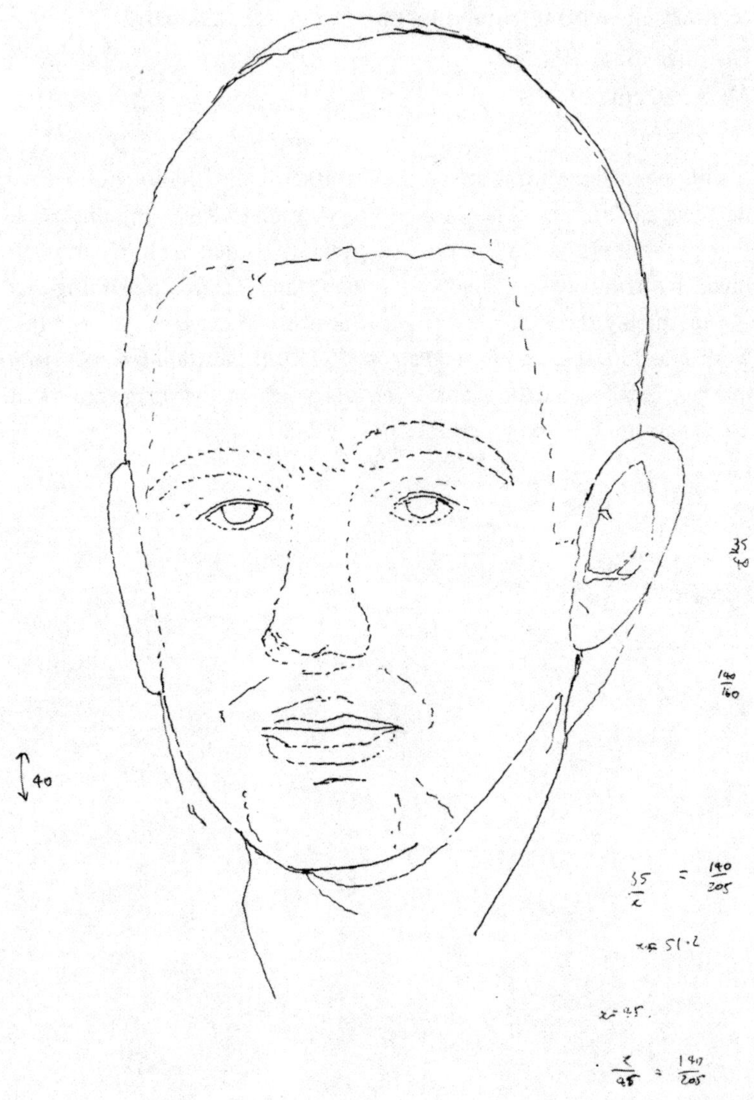

35
40
140
160
40
35
x
= 140
205
x = 51.2
x = 45
x
45
= 140
205

***Erased Portrait of Murray Bail* (1985)**

oilstick, oil, synthetic polymer paint on 67 canvasboards

No. 8075–8141

279 x 229 cm

In this painting, Murray's face is on the left-hand side of the picture near the superimposed canvasboard panel under a layer of paint. He is there but not visible. In fact I began this work by making him part of an image by Arthur Boyd, *Interior With Black Rabbit* (1973), a painting that Murray highly recommended to me. But in the process of painting this work, I decided that I preferred Fairweather's *Chi-tien Stands on His Head* instead. This became the visible layer. It is typical of my work process that failed paintings can be superseded or recycled.

***Portrait of an Australian* (1990)**
oilstick, gouache, synthetic polymer paint on 42 canvasboards
No. 30731–30772
229 x 178 cm

After my first (some would say) obscure and rather unsatisfying portrait, it was almost five years before this second attempt. At this time, Murray steered me in the rock-solid direction of Max Beckmann, a master of portraiture. In my work, Murray is brimming with confidence, reflecting the fact that his book on the New Zealand painter, Colin McCahon, was proceeding magnificently. Unfortunately this project soon afterwards ran aground on the dangerous rocks of New Zealand parochialism. I remember Helen Garner responding very positively to my version of Murray in my studio, even suggesting that Murray get a new haircut! This painting was subsequently a winner of the Aberdare Art Prize and is now in the Ipswich Art Gallery.

ORTRAIT
AN AUSTRALIAN

***Necessary Protection* (1990)**

gouache, oilstick, synthetic polymer paint on 42 canvasboards

No. 30816–30887

229 x 178 cm

This is probably the best and most successful portrait in the series and it was selected and hung in the 1990 Archibald Prize. The work is based on a snapshot Murray took while collecting data for his McCahon book. He generously gave me a number of these snapshots and I noticed that in one of them Murray's face and body were reflected in the glass protecting a work on paper by McCahon. It was as though Murray had been mapped into the McCahon itself through the act of photographing it. Also Murray's shadowy, reticent but nonetheless insistent presence is in stark contrast to the assertive 'I' of McCahon's work. Some friends even thought that Murray's elusive character had been finally captured here. What interested me most was the ready-made nature of this juxtaposition (captured inadvertently by Murray himself – not artificially engineered by me). I needed only to reproduce in a painting what was already present in the snapshot.

This work also came after two other ready-made portraits of other subjects – one of the filmmaker Paul Cox and one of my partner Jennifer Slatyer. When the work *My Wife as an Apparition* was hung in the Archibald Prize in 1989, the Sydney critic, John McDonald, suggested that I had superimposed Jennifer's face on a rather feeble nineteenth-century painting – the truth was that I had merely enlarged (using the superscan process) an existing work in its entirety. The uncanny resemblance to Jennifer was already there in the original – Isobel Tweddle's *Portrait of Miss Ivy Ball in Fancy Dress* – a work painted in the 1920s and now languishing in the vaults of the National Gallery of Victoria.

NECESSARY PROTECTION

***Untitled (1+1=3)* (1990)**

gouache, oilstick, synthetic polymer paint on 54 canvasboards

No. 31147–31200

229 x 229 cm

This work no longer exists. In fact I removed the twelve canvasboard panels featuring Murray and moved them to another painting – the fifth portrait, *The Return of Ulysses*. The remaining panels featuring the equations which don't add up became a new work called *Solutions*.

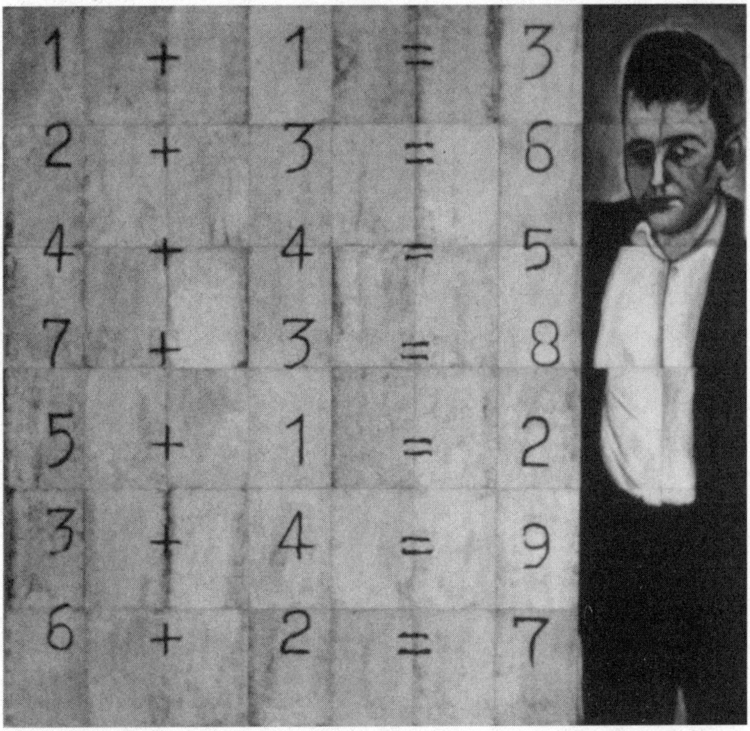
1 + 1 = 3
2 + 3 = 6
4 + 4 = 5
7 + 3 = 8
5 + 1 = 2
3 + 4 = 9
6 + 2 = 7

The Return of Ulysses (1991)

oilstick, gouache, synthetic polymer paint on 80 canvasboards

No. 33487–33566

254 x 305 cm

This is the last work of the series. Jennifer Slatyer has written that this work is a kind of homage to Murray Bail (and it is) through the inclusion of his silvery face, hovering God-like over the poignant scene depicted by de Chirico heeding Nietzsche's command to the artist 'to go back over everything that had already been done (the constant revisitation, the vicious circle, the serpent of time that bites its own tail in the cycle of eternity)'.

Or from a different point of view, is the Murray here like Giorgio de Chirico's alter ego – the wandering Ulysses returning to Penelope in the troubled tranquilly of a metaphysical interior?

First published in HEAT, *no. 8, 1998, pp. 97–109*

When Locality Prevails
2004

Everything pushes towards landscape
Philipp Otto Runge

Since we moved to this (some would say) godforsaken, bleak, arid, treeless landscape called the Monaro nearly eight years ago, an awareness of landscape has become inescapable to me. Every journey, on foot or by bus, car or aeroplane, entails contact with the austere local vistas of a landscape tempered by heat, frost, drought and decomposing granite. Here I have come to understand what Thomas Bernhard meant when he described gardening 'in all its possible and impossible forms'.

Naturally, issues of locality and identity have become uppermost in my mind and have made their presence felt in my recent work, not as literal representations of landscape, of the grass, hills, sky, clouds or rocks around me, but as *evocations*, through text and other layered visual elements. I have also been attracted to the ready-made poetry of the names of towns and localities and geographical features in my vicinity. For example in *Nature Speaks: AT* (2002), Bunyan, Polo Flat, Four Mile, Coolringdon, The Arable Road, The Brothers, The 'Jenny' Brothers, Kybeyan and Nimmitabel refer to actual sites in and around Cooma.

Being here has reinforced my interest in Aboriginal art, still the most powerful discourse within Australian art, and proof of the power of Joseph Beuys' dictum, 'Every human being an artist'. I strive to connect with this important art, which draws essentially on responses to the landscape. One approach I have taken is to collaborate with the Warlpiri artist Michael Nelson Jagamara. *Nature Speaks: AX* (2002) is one example of this. I dream and speculate on an enthusiastic response to Aboriginal art which one could call 'post-Aboriginal'.

I began the 'Nature Speaks' series in September 1998, and have completed eighty-nine works. With one exception, each consists of sixteen canvasboard panels arranged in a 4 x 4 grid. My goal, now not far from reach, is to complete 100 works.[1]

At first glance the series appears to proceed like an *algorithm* because of the repetition of certain elements within each work – like the word 'horizon'; the Mallarméan mantra 'A throw of the dice will never abolish chance'; the Tau cross of Colin McCahon's 'load-bearing structures'; and the ubiquitous cherubim of Philipp Otto Runge, from his unfinished *Gesamtkunstwerk* 'The Times of Day'.

There is also room for deviations, digressions, coincidences. *Nature Speaks: BK* (2004) is one such instance, inspired by a trip to Uluru and Kata Tjuta in 2000, which subsequently had a peculiarly *local* resonance for me. I discovered later that a fairly unremarkable outcrop of lichen-covered rocks surrounded by native *callitris* pines and overlooking the southern approach to Cooma was also named Ayers Rock. I pondered the mystery of this enigma: with the return of the *real* Ayers Rock to its Aboriginal custodians and the change of name to Uluru, it seemed as if its former name had somehow migrated or been displaced to the south-east of New South Wales – to Cooma. The 'Nature Speaks' series is always alert to such displacements, and attentive to enigmas.

Paradoxically the move to Cooma was more than a move to the grasslands of the Monaro. It gave me the opportunity to live and work in an old European-style garden of hundred-year-old pines, cedars and deciduous trees, including mature silver poplars, elms, prunus, crabapples and birches, and to experience fully the four seasons, what Runge calls 'the year in its successive states – blossoming, producing, bearing and destroying'. A European rhythm significantly different from that of the Australian landscape, yet still somehow within it. Here, in the garden at Blairgowrie, nature speaks in the Latvian vernacular of my childhood. As the Latvian poet Ilze Kalnāre describes it:

Runā akmens, runā kalns
Runā vārpus druvā
Runā katrs koks un lauks
Valodā tik tuvā.

The rock speaks, the mountain speaks
every ear of corn speaks
every tree and field, in a language
so intimate and familiar.

Philipp Otto Runge, writing in the early nineteenth century, not far from the shores of the Baltic Sea, echoes this sentiment:

There are times when it seems to me as if the world was splitting up into its individual elements, and as if the land, water, flowers, clouds, the moon and rocks were all conversing with one another. They all seem to be alive, and I start to feel half crazy; but I am patient and when I can get outside again I understand everything better.

Notes

1 I have now completed 290 'Nature Speaks' paintings.

First published in HEAT, *no. 8 new series, 2004, pp. 113–128*

Imants Tillers Discusses *Terra Incognita* and *Terra Negata* 2006

As Heiner Bastian has pointed out, Mallarmé wanted to write poetry similar in concept to the composition of a painting: 'Painting – not the thing, but the effect it creates. Verse should not be composed of words, but of intentions, and should destroy all words for the sake of sensation.' Thus the meaning of a poem can only be evoked by an *inner reflection of the words themselves*.

In my own works, particularly over the last decade, words, phrases and sentences (some of which come from Mallarmé) float not on the white space of a page, but in and amongst the colours, the forms and the imagery of a painting. As in Mallarmé, they are not there to be decoded, to arrive at a precise meaning predetermined by the author or the artist but rather to generate allusions and sensations in the reader/viewer.

During the 1980s I was very fortunate to be making frequent visits to New York and on several notable occasions I found myself standing in front of one of Jasper Johns's masterpieces: *Map* (1961) in the collection of the Museum of Modern Art. What appealed to me particularly was how the structure of the boundaries and names of the fifty-two states of the United States (together sometimes with adjoining bits of Canada and Mexico) allowed Johns a new kind of freedom with his gestural brushstrokes. Here, by virtue of some novel constraints, the Abstract Expressionism of de Kooning was given a new twist, a new life and a new relevance. It is perhaps not surprising, given my postmodern bent at the time, that this work gave me the idea of doing my own series of Johns's 'maps' (both the paintings and the prints), a repainting and reconfiguring of his work from an Antipodean viewpoint. I only completed two works: *Prophecy* (1989) and *Mystic America* (1989) which I exhibited in my fourth and last solo exhibition at the Bess Cutler Gallery in New York in 1989. (Bess was disappointed that neither work contained the name of her birthplace: Saskatchewan.)

Subsequently I experimented with the map of Australia but found its contour too distinctive and its subdivisions too few and too plain. It was only with the discovery of David Horton's *Map of Aboriginal Australia* at the beginning of the new millennium that I found a way to go forward on this front – for here was not only an alternative map to the familiar, boring one I had grown up with at school, but the 460 subdivisions demonstrated the rich diversity of the language/tribal/nation groups of the Indigenous people of Australia – a fact which had been largely invisible or unknown to most white Australians and the rest of the world. Here also, was the palpable lie to the misguided colonial idea of *terra nullius* – the so-called empty, unoccupied continent of 1788. While the regional divisions on Horton's map were panoramic, diverse and fascinating (the Northwest, Southwest, Desert, Spencer, Kimberley, North Arnhem, Fitzmaurice, Gulf, West Cape, Torres Strait, East Cape, Rainforest, Northeast, Eyre, Riverine, Southeast and Tasmania to name them all), it was the individual names themselves that most attracted me. I recognised words like Ngarigo, Arrernte, Luritja, Badjala, Wiradjuri, Adnyamathanha as a kind of eloquent ready-made poetry that I would like to include in my future paintings.

After about three years' work on this project I have completed two major paintings, both composed of 288 canvasboard panels and measuring 120" x 336" each: *Terra Incognita* in March

2005 and *Terra Negata* in November 2005. *Terra Incognita* is of a golden hue and described by my friend, the semiotician Anne Hénault, as being 'syntactical', while *Terra Negata* is of a red bronze hue and described as being 'paradigmatic'. In *Terra Incognita* I have isolated just the Aboriginal names themselves (without their defining boundaries) from Horton's map and distributed them spatially across the painting so that they correspond approximately to their actual geographical locations within the continent of Australia. In *Terra Negata* the same names are arranged in the form of an alphabetical list from A to Y, beginning with the name Alyawarre and ending with Yiman. The background image in both works – the tangled network or web of lines derives from a famous painting by the Aboriginal artist Emily Kame Kngwarreye who appeared on the art scene like a cloudburst in the early 1990s. Her *Big Yam Dreaming* (1995) in the National Gallery of Victoria in Melbourne is a work to rival *Blue Poles* or indeed the best of American Abstract Expressionism, be it Pollock or de Kooning. Furthermore, her painting is a kind of psychic and yet geographical mapping of the land, and in this has a strange and unexpected affinity with Jasper Johns's *Map* that once had me spellbound in New York.

Thus both *Terra Incognita* (shown for the first time in the 2006 exhibition *Imants Tillers: One World Many Visions* at the National Gallery of Australia) and *Terra Negata* (selected for the Sydney Biennale in 2006) are for me a kind of homage to Indigenous Australia, a lament for the tragedies of all the lost tribes, languages and cultures of Australia but also, simultaneously, a kind of honour roll for the spectacular resurgence of their culture. This has been revealed to the wider world largely through art and especially through the medium of painting – an amazing phenomenon to which all Australians have borne witness over the last thirty years.

First published in Artonview, *46, winter 2006, National Gallery of Australia, pp. 14–15.*

An Auspicious Entanglement
2012

Every individual is the centre of a system of emanation
Novalis

We are thrown into the world: to be enduring, to be abiding, to be issuing forth, to be emerging
Martin Heidegger

When I am painting on canvasboard panels, I work at a desk which I protect with discarded newspapers. It is the same desk that I sit at when writing or paying the bills. It has been like this, working on the same desk, for over thirty years. Firstly in Mosman, Sydney, and today in Blairgowrie, Cooma, looking through the large window of my studio into an old frosty homestead garden. When I began to work with the canvasboard panels (which, as the back of the Fredrix brand declares, have been 'serving artists around the world since 1868'), I decided to number all the panels consecutively from one to infinity. In 1981 I started with the numbers one to forty-nine in my very first canvasboard work, which I called *Suppressed Imagery*. Just now I have finished the work *Nature Speaks: DX* (the 217th work in the 'Nature Speaks' series), which is numbered 91,471 to 91,486.

In recent years, however, as text has become equally important to me as image, I sometimes find that words leap out from the newspapers protecting my desk, often from sections that I would never normally bother reading, like 'Drive', 'Professional' or 'Property', and I cut them out to use perhaps in future works.

I have become attracted to the ready-made poetry of sub-editors! 'Autumn a time of joy' is one such phrase that I have put into several paintings. Then there are tiny entries – brief news items or official notices that would never catch one's attention whilst reading the papers on a Saturday morning with a cup of coffee.

For example, there was this tragic story – like a vignette from a Thomas Bernhard anthology:

Miracle Over – MADRID: A man making a pilgrimage to say thank you to the 'Virgin of Miracles' for his survival in a road crash was killed when a car hit him. The 40-year-old truck driver was among pilgrims, including his two aunts, walking from his hometown of Ordes to Caion when he was hit.

Bernhard, the great Austrian author, loved to collect such gleanings from the daily Viennese newspapers to work up into darkly hilarious stories of lunacy, murder, character assassination, amnesia and suicide. The idiocy of the real.

Then, a few months later, this extraordinary item caught my attention as I was painting:

In Memoriam – Bardon, Geoffrey Robert AM. 2.8.1940–6.5.2003. In loving memory of our beloved husband and father – dearly loved and so sadly missed by wife Dorn, sons James and Michael and family. Always in our hearts and thoughts.

Of course, since it was in a discarded newspaper, protecting my desk, I had missed the actual anniversary of Bardon's death by two days: it had come to my attention on 8th May 2011.

Geoff Bardon, the school teacher and artist, was instrumental in stimulating the beginnings of the Papunya Tula art movement in 1971. As he wrote:

These Western Desert paintings seemed to me in 1971 to explicate and culturally enhance a visual writing in which word and image become one. The ideogrammatic and pictographic texts in these paintings were not understood linearly, but rather from any direction by the Western Desert peoples: They used an archetypal writing *summoned forth* from the brutal environment of the desert assimilationist camps and re-enacting the Western Desert culture in all its glory.

In 1986, I painted a work called *After Civilisation (for Geoff Bardon)*. It is a painting that has only ever been exhibited twice and never reproduced. It was first shown in the United States as part of a solo exhibition at a university gallery, *Australian Appropriations: The Recent Paintings of Imants Tillers*, at the Vollum College Center Gallery, Reed College, Portland, Oregon, 1 February–8 March 1987. This followed my exhibition in the Arsenale at the 42nd Venice Biennale where I was representing Australia. The second time it was shown as part of *Balance 1990: Views, Visions, Influences*, at the Queensland Art Gallery, Brisbane – a landmark exhibition coordinated by Michael Eather and Marlene Hall. The painting depicts a cosy living room with a red couch and green velvet drapes, looking out onto a classical landscape complete with Greek columns and temple ruins (based on a composition by Giorgio de Chirico). However, both room and landscape seem to have been infiltrated by Aboriginal energy!

The 'Aboriginal energy' is due to my quotation of Michael Nelson

Jagamara's winning design for the Parliament House Mosaic (one of the masterpieces of Australian art), reproduced ten years later on the cover of Vivien Johnson's monograph on Jagamara. Given past events and misunderstandings, Michael Eather and I sought Michael Nelson's permission to include this hitherto little-known painting of mine in the present exhibition. On the eve of his solo exhibition at FireWorks Gallery on 15 June 2012, Michael Nelson Jagamara gave his approval. As the poet Novalis once wrote: 'One is exalted for having received permission to do so from a person you were obliged to ask.'

There can be no doubt that the *only* original contribution Australia has made to the history of world art in the twentieth century is Australian Indigenous art, which begins with the Papunya Tula movement in 1971. A recent publication from Thames & Hudson, *Art: The Whole Story* (2010), edited by Stephen Farthing, bears this out most graphically, as this is indeed the only Australian entry in this comprehensive survey from 75,000 B.C.E. to the present. Aboriginal rock and cave paintings also feature in the earliest parts of this book – but it is the twentieth century that is of particular interest. This is not to deny, of course, outstanding non-Indigenous artists from the Antipodes such as John Peter Russell, Ian Fairweather, Fred Williams, Sidney Nolan, Colin McCahon or Ian Burn, amongst others, who deserve recognition on the world stage, but who nevertheless would count as part of other art movements, originating from elsewhere – Impressionism, Expressionism, Abstract Expressionism, Conceptual Art, etc. The originality of Australian Indigenous Art therefore stands alone.

In 1985, I painted a controversial work *The Nine Shots*, which drew its imagery from both Michael Nelson Jagamara and the German neo-expressionist Georg Baselitz. The process was not that of a simple overlay of one image over another but a more complex interspersal of both sources that involved a certain struggle to find what I felt was the right fit between them. Panels were removed, repainted, reassembled, rearranged to strike the right balance. Naïve and inexperienced, however, in Aboriginal culture and its protocols, my borrowing and transformation of motifs from Michael Nelson Jagamara's stunning work *Five Dreamings* (1984) were unauthorised, hence the controversy. However, as Novalis writes: 'Error is the indispensable instrument of truth. With error I make truth. The complete employment of error equals the complete possession of truth.'

Subsequently, *The Nine Shots* has arguably become my most successful and celebrated work, in so far as it is the most reproduced – illustrated in many Australian and international publications, it even appears as a footnote to the substantial entry (by Ian Mclean) on Michael Nelson Jagamara in *Art: The Whole Story*.

In *The Nine Shots*, the work I quoted from Baselitz was his painting *Forward Wind* (1965), which shows a man in front of a tree with outstretched arms, fixed to the tree. Crucified. In other works of Baselitz from this period, the tree is depicted alone, 'assuming a human form, rooted in the ground and stretching out its branches toward the sky, bleeding from the wounds dealt by fate'. In the 1980s, when I was exploring a new vocabulary of images for myself, I was particularly attracted to Baselitz's 'A New Type' series of 1965 and 1966, and I painted many paintings which included a range of these figures, in addition to the one in *The Nine Shots*.

Gunther Gercken, in a small catalogue of Baselitz's 'Hero

Paintings' for an exhibition at MW Gallery, New York, in 1990, has pointed out the distinguishing *marks* of these figures:

Youthful male figure, mostly standing, but sometimes seated or squatting...of gigantic stature, stressed by his small head and large hands, which display stigmata and hold a flag or palette, or carry a burning house or a wheelbarrow on an outstretched palm. Barefoot. The weight of his massive body is held in suspense by a forward movement that remains frozen.

Gercken described the *attitude* of this new type as 'of rapt emotion; of being overwhelmed without violence, of surrender; of suffering', and his *gaze* as 'ecstatic, prophetic, faraway, into the future'. The clothing of the new type is also noted: 'Battledress, open blouse with patch pockets, wide shorts or long pants gathered at the ankles, with bandages'.

Why was I drawn to these rather dismal figures? In the 1980s they seemed to hold some kind of truth for me that I had no means of accessing at that time. I proceeded by intuition. Now I think I recognise my deceased father, also named Imants Tillers, in these figures. Certainly his physical appearance and demeanour. I know that he was recruited to the Latvian Legion in 1943 when he was only seventeen or eighteen, in the period when Latvia was occupied by Nazi Germany, and that he was a prisoner of war of the Allies for a year in Belgium, firstly under the British and then the Americans, who set him and the other Latvians free. He met my mother in a displaced persons camp in Germany after the war, and my parents travelled in the ship *Volendam* to Australia as refugees, arriving in Sydney in 1949, the year before my birth.

Since my parents died (my father died in 2001, soon after the terrorist attacks on the United States; my mother in 2007), I have come into possession of a small number of tattered diaries that my father kept as a soldier and as a prisoner of war. They are highly emotionally charged objects, written in pencil in a neat handwriting on poor paper – in Latvian that defies my attempts at transcription and translation. I can barely imagine his sense of desolation. The great calamity that has befallen him. Hardly an adult. Not a shred of hope! Stupefied by circumstance. A victim of what is infinitely close at hand.

Nevertheless, from the diary, which contains elegant diagrams of his journey, I discover that he left Riga by ship on 19 August 1944, and was in Berlin on 18 February 1945 and Hannover on 2 March 1945. In between, there were seven journeys on foot – 'the walks of failure' – and other train journeys. These journeys to nowhere seem to finish on 9 September 1945 – the places are unrecognisable (and incomprehensible) to me: Kehele, Booma, Brigge, Zedelgema. As Thomas Bernhard writes in *On the Mountain*: 'Alone with our destination, with our father and with our mother.'

The chocolate box – Lindt Lindor Assorted – in which my mother kept my father's diaries, contains a single handwritten note in my wife Jennifer's handwriting:

Hohn in 1947 – hamlet in Germany where Dzidra and Imants were married, near Hamlin (the region) – in May the streets were lined with apple trees in blossom – they married a year after meeting when they were housed in accommodation for displaced persons in houses belonging to people who'd fled.

In one of the diaries there is another poignant entry – two addresses: one in Chicago; the other, somewhere in Argentina. Nevertheless, my father survived the war, met my mother and came to Australia, where there was no one waiting for them. And their first-born son, of Latvian heritage, also an Imants, went on to collaborate with a Warlpiri artist who lived in the Western Desert. Who could have envisaged such an unlikely chain of events?

Novalis: 'Friends, the ground is poor; we must strew abundant seed that we might nonetheless reap a modest harvest.'

What can I say about the collaborations with Michael Nelson Jagamara? They were conducted over vast distances. There is much terrain between the southern tablelands in New South Wales, the plateau called the Monaro into which the town of Cooma nestles, the government settlement of Papunya in Central Australia (where Michael Nelson Jagamara still lives and works, and where Albert Namatjira served his detention in 1959 just before his death), and the city of Brisbane on Queensland's south-eastern coast – the home of Michael Eather, FireWorks Gallery and the Campfire Group. The triangle of doubt – but also of great possibilities.

From the outset, we wanted to limit the number of joint works – and there were only seven works painted between 2001 and 2008. Seven works over seven years. It is a very modest harvest! But it allowed me to investigate issues to do with chance, destiny, poetic knowledge, history, identity and Aboriginality in other works of my own. During this period, I became fascinated with the uncanny resonance, for example, between the works of another of Australia's great artists, Emily Kngwarreye, and the American painter Brice Marden, whose work can at other times resemble that of Ian Fairweather and even Fred Williams.

But in particular I studied the works of Emily Kngwarreye. As Novalis has said: 'only an artist can divine the sense of life. The genuine poet is all knowing – he is an actual world in miniature.' In the works of Emily Kngwarreye, one can discern the kind of poetic knowledge that Novalis is referring to when he writes: 'The consummate form of knowledge must be poetic. Each theorem must have an individual character – it must be a self-evident individuum enveloping a flash of insight'. While Emily Kngwarreye paints rather than writes – the paintings all contain a story, or fragments of a story. Novalis: 'As in Taoism...the less the artist exists as a being separate from his work, the more perfect the work. See for instance, Chuang Tsu's tale of the woodcarver, in which the woodcarver simply allows the work to appear in its perfection'. Is this not a profound insight if applied to Emily Kngwarreye's paintings?

In 2005, I painted two memorials to Aboriginal Australia – *Terra Incognita*, which is on display at the National Gallery of Australia in Canberra; and *Terra Negata*, which I have included in this exhibition. Both works quote extensively from one of the great works of the twentieth century – Emily Kngwarreye's *Big Yam Dreaming* (1995). They acknowledge in different ways the historical occupation of Australia by Aboriginal peoples before colonisation, by drawing on the evidence of David Horton's map, which shows the distribution of over 460 Aboriginal tribal/language groups across the Australian continent. I intended these two works to be a refutation of the once convenient but bizarre doctrine of *terrra nullius*. I cannot imagine these works being painted had I not been immersed in a process of collaboration with Michael Nelson Jagamara.

Another point about the collaborations is that Michael Nelson, in a conspicuous spirit of goodwill, agreed to the works being painted on canvasboard panels, being numbered and included as part of my so-called *Book of Power*. Yet they are still part of his oeuvre as well. Michael Nelson Jagamara, whenever he has been faced with a new challenge in the artistic arena, is known 'to have a go'. He is not only one of the great Aboriginal artists, but certainly the most *experimental* of them all. Most recently, when I was asked by Torah Bright, the Cooma snowboarder who won gold for Australia at the last winter Olympics, to decorate her 2012 snowboard – the Roxy Bright 'Eminence' Edition – I invited Michael Nelson to collaborate as well. So the final design contains a 'lightning dreaming'. Michael Nelson Jagamara must be the first Aboriginal artist to feature on a snowboard!

None of these collaborations with Michael Nelson Jagamara could have taken place without the involvement of Michael Eather. To him I am very grateful. His understandings of and engagement with Aboriginal people have allowed him to create a truly experimental situation in Brisbane, particularly the Campfire Group but now with FireWorks Gallery as well. It was his idea to suggest that Michael Nelson and I work on 'a couple of collaborative paintings' when my attempt in 2001 to involve Michael Nelson Jagamara in a sculptural project at Overflow Park at the Olympic site at Homebush Bay in Sydney fell through.

During the course of seven years of intermittent engagement with Michael Nelson, I remember visiting Michael Eather's house in Brisbane for dinner on one occasion. Michael Nelson Jagamara was staying there, downstairs with another Aboriginal artist. Both were in Brisbane to work on paintings.

'What do they do when they are downstairs?' I asked. 'They're watching the Nature Channel on cable TV,' replied Michael. Then I noticed a cloud of flying ants around the light above the dinner table. 'Due to Michael Nelson Jagamara's presence downstairs,' laughed my host. Today I understand that Flying Ant Dreaming (the subject of one of Michael Nelson's first paintings in 1979) is better explained by saying 'spirit-being called Flying Ant'.

Novalis: 'Bringing forth the world. Every word is a word of incantation. Whatever spirit is called, such a one appears. Blossoming flame, speaking flame, changing flame'.

Then there was a remarkable phone call from Michael Nelson Jagamara from a public telephone box in Papunya to me in Cooma. I was quite taken aback! It was not about our collaborations but on another subject. That is the only telephone call I have ever received from Papunya.

On another occasion, there was an encounter with possums or perhaps a spirit-being named Possum. I was working on the fourth work in the collaborative series, *From Afar* (2002), which contained a Possum Dreaming by Michael Nelson as an underlayer. One night when we were not at home, a possum came down the narrow flue of our kitchen slow-combustion stove. It was covered in black soot and wreaked havoc through several adjoining rooms until it passed through the studio. On the floor was the unfinished painting *From Afar*, and the possum chose to walk across it, leaving its black possum prints in the bottom left-hand corner.

The work already contained the strange, unfathomable words of the Japanese-American artist Shusaku Arakawa: 'The distance out of which, who, repeatedly hypostatised speaks'. I was astonished by the possum prints but eventually painted over them – adding the words ‘confused possum’ to mark their former presence.

Four years have elapsed since the seventh and final collaborative work, *Fatherland* (2008), was completed. Now it is over ten years since Michael Nelson and I first embarked on our adventure, and early last year, Michael Eather told me that Michael Nelson was not satisfied with only seven works and was eager to do more. So the thought came to me to do a very large work that could be both a celebration of the Papunya Tula movement and also a lamentation for its twilight – since many of the original artists have become old or have already passed away. *Hymn to the Night* was chosen as a working title. It references an epic poem by Novalis:

Downwards I turn
Towards the holy, unspeakable,
Mysterious Night.

The idea for the painting developed over a year and was completed by Michael Nelson on 20 March this year. It is painted on 165 canvasboard panels and measures approximately 3 x 5 metres. If the first seven collaborative works constitute the first chapter, *Hymn to the Night* perhaps heralds the beginning of the second – another path – and perhaps Novalis should be our guide and talisman on this second journey.

Novalis was the pen-name of the German romantic poet and visionary philosopher Friedrich von Hardenberg (1772–1801), who before his untimely death compiled notes for an encyclopedia of universal knowledge, on topics ranging from the natural world to mystical religion.

As the translator of a recent compilation of Novalis’ writings,

Fragments and Pollen, Arthur Versluis points out 'that his work is a compelling synthesis of natural philosophy and mythic imagination, which awakens us to the reality that Nature is a spiritual poem and that human and cosmic love are ultimately one'. As Novalis writes: 'Since God was able to become man, he can become even stones, plants, animals and elements and perhaps there is in this way a perpetual deliverance in nature.'

Before Michael Nelson touched any of the canvasboard panels, I was marking out a 'ghost version' of *Hymn to the Night* in Cooma on a second set of 165 panels. My text was a kind of poetic map of the Western Desert and its inhabitants – with Papunya at its heart. Also, I included words about 'surrender' and 'extinction'. These mainly come from the Australian playwright Janis Balodis (who is also of Latvian heritage):

We surrendered our land
we surrendered our history
we surrendered our culture
we surrendered our souls
we surrendered our language
we surrendered our children
we surrendered our hope
we surrendered our lives
we surrendered our identity
    and yet...

He was referring to Latvians under the long years of Soviet occupation – from 1944 to 1991. Equally he might have been speaking from the point of view of all the lost Aboriginal tribes, which once occupied the entire continent of Australia.

Hymn to the Night marks a change in the methodology of our collaborative process. In this work, I surrender to Michael Nelson Jagamara. He both started and finished this work. My layer (a background of colours that 'speak') is sandwiched between his beginning and his end. Michael Nelson understands the intention of this work – its content of mourning for the passing generations – the brilliant but fleeting moment of Papunya Tula. However, why not see these inevitable changes as the catalyst for the dawn of a new kind of art in the twenty-first century, one that might be called 'post-Aboriginal'. A unique synthesis of the old and the new – the Aboriginal and the contemporary. And who else to lead the way but someone like Michael Nelson Jagamara? One of the original artists in the second wave of the movement in the 1970s and perhaps the individual who is most receptive to contemporary modes of art – certainly one of the most experimental!

The fact of our collaboration in an ongoing series of canvasboard works since 2001 is remarkable, and it is indeed a great privilege for me to continue to be a part of it. For us, 'the miracle' is not over yet.

I have been recognised as an artist for forty years now. And as I reflect on the passing years, I see each decade being characterised by a unique emphasis or theme. I would suggest that they trace the following trajectory or sequence: post-object; postmodern; post-Soviet (or postcolonial); post-Aboriginal. I describe the way, and meanwhile, perhaps, I am proceeding along it.

First published in The Loaded Ground: Michael Nelson Jagamara & Imants Tillers, *ANU Drill Hall Gallery, Canberra, 2012.*

Introduction to *Artist's Choice*
2016

The noted American artist Edward Hopper once remarked, 'if I could say it in words there would be no reason to paint', thus reinforcing the widespread prejudice that *artists should be seen and not heard*.[1] Yet in this book we have a compilation of artists' writings on other artists. Here the artists are not just permitted, but invited, to speak.

Giorgio de Chirico, one of the greatest artists of the twentieth century, was also a fine writer. He wrote over seventy articles and essays on various topics between 1914 and 1973 as well as the acknowledged surrealist masterpiece *Hebdomeros* in 1929. And then there are his highly entertaining *Memoirs*, compiled 'in a vein of militant egocentricity'.[2] So too I enjoyed Sidney Nolan's writings and poetry in the book *Nolan on Nolan: Sidney Nolan in His Own Words* (2007) edited by Nancy Underhill. There are some wonderful lines in it – 'Being Liars they called it paradise' – among others.[3] Also, on looking in the index, I was surprised to find that 'Imants Tillers' is referred to on page 350. Moreover, on the evidence of this current publication, an assemblage of Artist's Choices from the pages of *Art & Australia* from 1967 to 2014, artists not only bring fresh insights to the work of other artists but also can give voice to these insights in eloquent and distinctive prose.

The first Artist's Choice in *Art & Australia* was published in the 1967 summer issue. In it, John Olsen produced a short, lyrical, heartfelt text about the painting *The Road to Berry* (1947) by Lloyd Rees. He describes *The Road to Berry* as 'full of the buttery warmness that Rees painted for himself in the early 1940s'. Also how Rees learned through 'cobwebby analysis', that 'less is more' and how, eschewing the palette of the impressionists, 'he preferred sombre elegiac tonalities that included a feeling of warm earth regretfully saying farewell to an evening sky'. Here, Olsen seeks to rehabilitate the reputation of an artist whose star seems to be fading; above all, he extols Rees's virtue of resisting fashion – instead seeking 'his personal paradise'. There is a strategic dimension to the time of Olsen's text since a new generation of hip young artists who had embraced the international styles of hard-edge and colour field painting were about to be launched in the watershed exhibition 'The Field' at the National Gallery of Victoria, Melbourne, in the following year.

It was twelve years later, in 1979, that *Art & Australia* published the second Artist's Choice, which was Jeffrey Smart writing on Brian Dunlop's painting *Room* (1978), in which he praises the Art Gallery of New South Wales, Sydney, for purchasing this work against the prevailing art fashions of the time. Smart's text is a thoughtful meditation on both the painting and on Dunlop's path to becoming an artist.

My own Artist's Choice in 1981 was the seventh in the series, and by then *Art & Australia* had fully embraced Artist's Choice as an ongoing feature of the magazine. While my text purportedly focuses on Tom Roberts's painting *Impression* (now *Mentone*, 1888) it is not about the content of the Roberts painting, nor the way it is painted, nor about his oeuvre per se but rather the photomechanical reproduction of images in general and the distortions and transformations of the 'original' which can and do occur. I wrote this piece because I'd just used that particular Roberts painting as the starting point for a work of my own. Hence,

I particularly enjoyed reading Shaun Gladwell's very witty take from 2013 on Mike Parr's sculpture *Untitled* (1988) 'a giant wedge rising from the cut grass' beside the AGNSW, which he uses as launch ramp for his skateboarding exploits. As he wrote: it is an object 'screaming to be jumped from' – 'the *traceur* and *traceuse* of parkour will read it as a runway to the sky'.

Incidentally I had to look up the meaning of 'parkour' – evidently it is 'a holistic training discipline created in France'. [4] So too I was bemused to come across the word 'oogmerk' in Mike Parr's text from 2004 on Derek Kreckler's work *Holey I* (2003).[5] Parr's piece is a brilliant tour de force of creative interpretation. As he wrote: 'In both photographs the central figure of a man, his lower body wrapped in a turquoise towel, looks out to sea, unmoving, large, a sort of *oogmerk*'.

Other highlights, and there are many, include John Young's text from 1998 in which he shares an intimate moment from his personal life with us. 'I have chosen *Two women in a landscape*, painted by David Strachan in 1968, or rather the painting chose me, at a moment when my companion and wife is expecting a child'. Also I loved Rosalie Gascoigne's 1984 text on one of the great paintings on permanent display in Australia – Colin McCahon's *Victory Over Death 2* (1970) in which she tells us that she never pays 'even a fleeting visit to the Australian National Gallery without going in to see how [this painting] is getting along. And it is, as ever, getting along just fine'. Equally, I was moved by Madonna Staunton's almost mystical reverie on Ian Fairweather's *Epiphany* (1962). Then there are diverting revelations for the reader in Judy Cassab's beautiful farewell to her friend Stanislaus Rapotec; Tracey Moffatt on a disturbing photograph by Russell Drysdale;

Destiny Deacon's piece on Grace Crowley ('Okay, I picked out this charming painting on a whim'); and Simryn Gill's meditation on an Indian miniature from two centuries ago by Bulaki ('Who was Bulaki? The artist in me wants to know'). Of course there are many more Artist's Choices here, equally fascinating.

What is missing, however, from this volume is a work by Giorgio de Chirico. And in 1981 when I was given my chance to write there were no de Chirico paintings in any public collections in Australia. By 2013 this situation had been rectified and there are now two! Given the chance to nominate one of these I would choose the painting once titled *Antique Horses* (1963) but now called *The Divine Horses of Achilles, Balios and Xanthos* (1963). It is a 'late' de Chirico. For many years it was part of Giorgio de Chirico and Isabella Far's personal collection in Rome and was even included in the exhibition 'De Chirico by de Chirico' at the New York Cultural Center in 1972. Now it can be seen at the AGNSW. For the catalogue of the New York exhibition, de Chirico wrote his own notes in his distinctive handwriting and in his French voice (!) on each page, next to each reproduced image. It looks as though someone (de Chirico) has 'corrected' or 'defaced' a printed catalogue that has been given to him by another. About the Sydney painting he wrote:

> O ruins Temples of Neptune invaded by the sea waves pushing the dolphins up to the sanctuary where, in normal times, even the initiated would enter trembling, holding his sandals in his hand.[6]

Perhaps if de Chirico had been asked to make an Artist's Choice by *Art & Australia* he might have selected this very painting. For as Robert Pincus-Witten wrote in 1984 with a certain irony: 'Giorgio de Chirico arguably is the greatest artist of the twentieth century – a hypothesis that de Chirico himself tirelessly put forth.'[7]

Nevertheless the artists' voices assembled in this compelling, entertaining and informative volume span over four decades and reflect not only the changing narrative of the Australian art world but the different viewpoints of the various editors of *Art & Australia* over this long period. There are fascinating insights, tributes and responses to major Australian and international artists whose works are to be found in Australian collections – an editorial guideline over the years that was adhered to obediently I believe, except for Ken Whisson's piece on Paul Klee in 2003, Nicholas Harding's on a painting by Goya in 2006, and Simryn Gill's 2013 text on Bulaki's miniature. While this guideline in retrospect might seem like an unnecessary, even parochial, restriction, it is what lends this collection its unique, authentic and local flavour. I found that all the texts are sincere and written in good faith – reminding me that looking at art that moves you confirms the value of art and the worthiness of being an artist. This book is a celebration of art and artists.

Notes

1. Quote from Hopper seen on a black carry bag for the Arts and Health conference at the National Gallery of Australia, (November 2011).
2. Giorgio de Chirico, *The Memoirs of Giorgio de Chirico* (New York: Da Capo Press, 1994).
3. Nancy Underhill ed., *Nolan on Nolan: Sidney Nolan in His Own Words* (Victoria: Penguin Group Australia, 2007), p. 425.
4. According to the online dictionary <http://dictionary.reference.com/>, it is 'a sport or activity of running through urban areas while performing various gymnastic manoeuvres over or on manmade obstacles such as walls and buildings'.
5. A Dutch word, *oogmerk* means 'purpose' or 'with a view to', 'with the intention of' or 'for the purpose of' – for example 'he took the computer with a view to pawning it'.
6. Giorgio de Chirico, *De Chirico by de Chirico,* New York Cultural Centre, New York, and Art Gallery of Ontario, Toronto, 1972, p. 70.
7. Robert Pincus-Witten, *De Chirico: Post-Metaphysical and Baroque Paintings,* Robert Miller Gallery, New York, 1984, unpaginated.

First published in Artist's Choice: Five Decades of Artists' Writing, Essays From Art & Australia 1967–2014 (2016).

Metafisica Australe
2017

When Giorgio de Chirico died in 1978, Japanese-American artist Shusaku Arakawa wrote a brief, somewhat enigmatic tribute to him. This note was passed on to me and I took notice because while I knew little about de Chirico at the time, I knew quite a lot about Arakawa.

In the early 1970s, I produced a work entitled *Still Life 2*, a black box containing an array of boxed elements, which was exhibited as part of my first solo exhibition, *Moments of Inertia* at Watters Gallery, Sydney, in 1973. It was pointed out to me then that this work had affinities to the work of Marcel Duchamp. Totally ignorant of Duchamp's work, I conducted an intensive study. I was particularly drawn to his celebrated work *The Bride Stripped Bare by Her Bachelors, Even* (1915–23), also known as *The Large Glass*. Needless to say, I pored over the contents of *The Green Box* (1934), Duchamp's notes and projects for *The Large Glass*. I tried to fathom the unfathomable.

Around this time I also noticed, in a catalogue of art books, one with a very compelling title, *The Mechanism of Meaning*, by Arakawa and Madeline Gins.[1] I obtained the first edition, only available in German, published in Munich in 1971; one had to wait until 1979 for the first English edition. Nevertheless *The Mechanism of Meaning* together with *The Large Glass* came to occupy my mind in the 1970s. Michael Govan, who curated the Arakawa and Gins retrospective titled *Reversible Destiny* for the Guggenheim Museum in New York in 1997, describes *The Mechanism of Meaning* (which was both a publication and a multi-panel cycle begun in 1963 and completed in large part by 1973), as 'a touchstone of conceptual art'.[2] Govan notes that Duchamp had said that through his own work he wanted 'to put art back at the service of the mind'. Arakawa, according to Govan, wanted art 'to question the very nature of the mind that contemplates it'. Legend has it that when Arakawa left Japan 'under a cloud', he arrived in New York in 1961 penniless, with only a scrap of paper with one phone number scrawled on it – that of Marcel Duchamp.[3] Soon after he met Duchamp they became friends, and by 1964 Arakawa had produced his own homage to Duchamp: *Diagram with Duchamp's Glass as a Minor Detail*.[4] Govan sees Arakawa as the natural heir to Duchamp's artistic legacy, rather than those other aspiring American bachelors of the time, John Cage, Jasper Johns, Robert Rauschenberg and Merce Cunningham, whom Arakawa knew very well. (Needless to say, this is not a popular view.)

So when on de Chirico's death, Arakawa sought to recuperate his reputation and draw attention to his profound importance, I listened. Arakawa's piece was entitled 'Towards Francis Picabia', written in New York City on 3 December 1978:

Just as Stephane Mallarmé was once maligned I am afraid that this too might be happening in our time to Giorgio di [sic] Chirico. Now as then this is ultimately not important at all. Despite foolish murmurings about such trivial matters as time, place and style within an enormous body of work, the artist pursues his intention.

After the great metaphysical discoveries, an even more magnificent one of a personal order, that is, what to do with these discoveries. He had almost no choice. Evidently, a rigorous epistemological study was required. So, unlike Marcel Duchamp, for example, he undertook such an investigation but completely hidden from view. In what he has been doing, there is almost no process which can be seen. Luckily I had some suspicions for a long time. Then recently I had a chance to meet him.

When we spoke about the so-called 'scandalous' dates, he replied: 'Why do people care so much about numbers? I can put any number I wish. Can't people distinguish between imitation and variation? Many artists make variations but when I make extremely exact variations people complain.' (Nearly totally exact in his variations which on such occasions hide a process of discovery which he internalizes.)

When asked by M. Gins, 'What is missing from this world?' he replied immediately: 'Morality, kindness and a sense of justice.'

Regarding the quality of layered transparency in his work, the important discovery he has written was 'no longer dried pigment, but coloured matter'.

During our conversation he emphasized:

'I hate lemons, but love lemon pies.'

These are only a few examples to roughly spell out a hidden process. This might be thought of as a private language in public terms. Giorgio di Chirico might paint anything supposedly easily recognisable to all but it is intended into his secret process not out to the viewer. Oddly this is completely a one-man show or act, nameless and unrecognizable at this time, but in the near future we will call it an effort toward the construction of a model of being, mind.[5]

In 1979 I visited New York with my wife Jennifer Slatyer for the first time. One fortunate and unexpected outcome was that we met Arakawa and Madeline Gins. It was not until the 1980s however, when I began to exhibit regularly in New York, that we formed a friendship. Arakawa described me as a 'very porous' character – no doubt because as an appropriation artist my work was potentially open to any and every influence – and told me I should rotate my canvasboard panels off the wall into space to create sculptural forms. I do this now, in a sense, when I exhibit two-dimensional elements with three-dimensional stacks of painted and unpainted panels. In any case, every individual work I produce, while it can stand alone, is also part of what I have called the *Book of Power* – an accumulating and evolving entity that consists of *all* the canvasboard panels I have ever painted since 1981. To emphasise this, each canvasboard has been consecutively numbered from one to infinity. At the time of writing, I am close to 100,000. The *Book of Power* could be an all-encompassing 'book', an 'inventory', a 'compendium', a 'system', a 'neural network' or maybe even, to use Arakawa's term, a crude 'model of being'.

Not long after I had absorbed 'Towards Francis Picabia', I came across the book *De Chirico*, introduced by his wife Isabella Far and published by Harry N. Abrams in 1968, in a second-hand bookshop. This must have been in the early 1980s – coincidentally, at the same time I became aware of the Papunya Tula art movement. Both bodies of work attracted me and I began to use imagery from each, mostly separately but by the mid-1980s they met in a handful of works, most significantly in *Antipodean Manifesto* (1986).

Antipodean Manifesto takes de Chirico's *Dead Sun in a Metaphysical Interior* (1971) as its starting point. (I've also seen this work titled, strangely, *Metaphysical Interior with Sun Turned Off*.) At the time, I paid no heed to the title or date but chose the image because I liked it, and I simply substituted the black void or abyss at its centre with a powerful symmetrical Papunya Tula motif. This motif was based on Paddy Carroll Tjungurrayi's *Witchetty Grub Ceremonies* (1983), which I'd come upon in a calendar! They seemed to fit perfectly together. Incidentally, I met Paddy Carroll by chance in 2002 when I began to collaborate with another Warlpiri artist, Michael Nelson Jagamara at the Campfire Studios associated with Michael Eather's FireWorks Gallery in Brisbane. The date of my source now seems a bit uncanny, for when de Chirico painted *Dead Sun in a Metaphysical Interior* in 1971 it was the exact same moment that the Papunya Tula movement began in the Western Desert. I'd selected de Chirico's image in 1986 not because of the significance of the date but because I felt it had some weird resonance with Aboriginal art.

Throughout the 1980s and into the 1990s, the work of de Chirico became one of my main points of reference. In 1986 when I represented Australia at the Venice Biennale, I brought back the seven volumes of the *Catalogo Generale Giorgio de Chirico*, each of which consists of three catalogues.[6] The first covers 1908–30, the second 1931–50 and the third 1951–72, so there are twenty-one catalogues altogether. The disconcerting thing about the catalogues is that, irrespective of the dates, each period seems to include the same diverse array of themes and subjects: in any volume we find examples of the early metaphysical paintings (some, of course, are variations of earlier paintings, such as *The Disquieting Muses* and the *Piazza d'Italia*); the classical still lifes; the anthropomorphic horses on the beach; the gladiators in a room; copies after the grand masters such as Michelangelo, Rubens, Titian, Veronese; the archaeologists and the mannequins; furniture in the valley; views of Venice; the mysterious bathers...and so on. The catalogues seem interchangeable, representing a vast oeuvre in which chronology is irrelevant – any of his varied themes can be potentially present at the same moment – thus *time* seems to have disappeared. This is in direct contrast to the teleological progression in modernism (from figuration to abstraction) in the work of artists such as Mondrian, Kandinsky, Rothko, Pollock and even New Zealander Colin McCahon. Giorgio de Chirico evokes the metaphysical realm where time does not exist, not only in certain individual works but in the totality of his oeuvre. In a letter to Apollinaire in 1916 he writes:

> It has been almost two years since I have seen you. The Ephesian teaches us that time does not exist, and that on the great curve of eternity the past is the same as the future. This might be what the Romans meant with their image of Janus, the god with two faces; and every night in dream, in the deepest hours of rest, the past and future appear to us as equal, memory blends with prophesy in a mysterious union.[7]

After decades of immersion in de Chirico's metaphysical project and following, in parallel, the phoenix-like rebirth of Aboriginal art from its moment of reinvention at Papunya, I had, in Venice in 2014, what my daughter Isidore describes as 'a breakfast epiphany'. It suddenly (or finally) occurred to me that perhaps all Aboriginal art is metaphysical – a term I had never seen before used in relation to Aboriginal art – and so there is a real connection with the metaphysical art of Giorgio de Chirico. I was then reminded of Antonin Artaud's realisation, 'the crucial thing is that we know that behind the order of this world there is another'.

Ian McLean, author of the recently published *Rattling Spears* and a highly respected authority on Indigenous art, was quick to confirm my somewhat vague intuition.[8] 'Australian Aboriginal art is deeply metaphysical,' he wrote. 'Its every empirical encounter with the world opens to a much larger cosmological reality, called "Dreaming". This is the link between it and the art of Giorgio de Chirico, the twentieth-century master of Western metaphysical painting.'[9] There was soon an opportunity in Rome to present this connection between de Chirico and Western Desert painting for the very first time.

Two French collectors of Western Desert painting, Marc Sordello and Francis Missana, secured the Carlo Bilotti Museum in Rome to show their collection, the Sordello Missana Collection. While this museum had an impressive program of temporary, mainly European, exhibitions, it also had an extensive collection of works by de Chirico on permanent view. But there was a question in the room – how could these works from the Antipodes have any meaning in Rome in the context of this museum? The guest curators for *Dreamings: Aboriginal Australian Art Meets de Chirico*, Ian McLean and Erica Izett, solved this problem by inviting me to exhibit seven works from the 1980s and the present that cited aspects of both Western Desert paintings and de Chirico's paintings, some of which combined both sources in the one image. I had a room of paintings next to a room of de Chirico paintings, forming a kind of bridge to the Aboriginal works downstairs. Quite incredibly, in the de Chirico room there were already two works with prior links to Australia: *Italian Piazza, Girl with Hoop* (1948), shown in *Surrealism: Revolution by Night* at the National Gallery of Australia in 1993, and *Self-Portrait with the Bust of Minerva* (undated), included in my exhibition *Diaspora in Context: Connections in a Fragmented World*, at the Museum of Contemporary Art in Sydney in 1995. Both works had once belonged to the distinguished public servant Dr Peter Wilenski, who had inherited them from a close relative – de Chirico's second wife, Isabella Far de Chirico! So, both works had spent time in the distant Antipodes – a place de Chirico never visited, but a place he may have sometimes imagined. Why else would the artist have inserted the word 'Melbourne' in his celebrated novel *Hebdomeros*? As Murray Bail puts it: 'The dreamy novel *Hebdomeros* was published in France in 1929. Unusually, it opens with the word 'And', then almost immediately gives poor Melbourne a kick in the teeth.'

> And then began the tour of that strange building situated in a street that looked forbidding, although it was distinguished and not gloomy. As seen from the street the building was reminiscent of a German consulate in Melbourne. Its ground floor was entirely taken up with large stores. Although it was neither Sunday nor a holiday, the stores were closed, endowing this part of the street with an air of tedium and melancholy, a certain desolation, that particular atmosphere which pervades Anglo-Saxon towns on Sundays.[10]

I first alluded to the remarkable presence of Melbourne in de Chirico's imagination in an essay titled 'Locality Fails' that I wrote for *Art & Text* in 1982.[11] Since then I've come across a reference to Melbourne in the work of Italo Calvino. In his *Cosmicomics*, a meditation on the nature of 'signs', he writes: 'one scratch out of eight hundred thousand on the creosoted wall between two docks in Melbourne'.[12] Maybe allusions to Melbourne continue to bounce around in Italian literature as a metaphor for boring remoteness and tedious irrelevance – a legacy of de Chirico, of which we here in the Antipodes are largely oblivious.

Speculation about Melbourne also occurs in the vast commentary about de Chirico's prodigious output in painting, sculpture and writing. An article by Antonella Sbrilli titled 'Album di Ebdòmero'[13] caught my eye, especially the first subtitle: 'Metafisica Australe'. A friend translated the Italian for me and I was able to deduce that the remote and exotic place 'Melbourne' entered de Chirico's imagination when he received a postcard of the Italianate Treasury Building in Melbourne (designed by T.J. Clark to house the bounty flowing from the Victorian goldfields) from his expatriate Roman friend Gino Nibbi: *Greetings from a Distant Friend*!

In 'Locality Fails' I made reference to Bell's Theorem, a startling discovery in quantum physics made by Belfast scientist John Bell in 1964 that 'proved Einstein wrong'. Bell's Theorem, more formally known as 'On the Einstein-Podolsky paradox', demonstrates that Einstein's views on quantum mechanics, the behaviour of very small things such as atoms and subatomic particles, were incorrect. Einstein had been sceptical from the outset about the theories of quantum mechanics pioneered by Niels Bohr, Werner Heisenberg and others: 'It seems hard to look at God's cards. But that he plays dice and uses telepathic methods (as the present quantum theory requires of him) is something I cannot believe for a moment.'[14]

Nevertheless, Bell's Theorem, which came after Einstein's death, continues to have an impact on modern physics and is said to have laid the foundation for quantum information technology, particularly indispensable today for use in the financial services and cyber-security industries. In the essay, I used Bell's counterintuitive principle of 'action at a distance' as a metaphor for cultural transmissions 'at a distance' to give hope to *us* distant Antipodean artists who *longed* to be noticed by the world at large. So, I was delighted to discover recently that, according to the world's leading scientific journal *Nature*, 'Bell's Theorem still reverberates'.[15] In 2016 it had not been disproved. Quantum entanglement still makes the impossible possible.

Unexpectedly, Bell's Theorem also continues to reverberate in my work – in the *Book of Power*, most recently with the unwitting assistance of artist Richard Bell. In 2001 at the invitation of Michael Eather, I began a collaborative relationship with Michael Nelson Jagamara at FireWorks Gallery, and it was here that I met a number of other artists from the gallery's stable, including Richard Bell. At this time Eather, demonstrating a generous spirit of comradeship, gave Richard a copy of Graham Coulter-Smith's freshly published book on my work, *The Postmodern Art of Imants Tillers: Appropriation en abyme, 1971–2001*, and Bell, being an inquisitive and intelligent man, read it.[16] It was here that he happily came upon the expression 'Bell's Theorem' and saw that he could adapt this reference to his own work and political agenda. Soon after he produced a painting on twenty-five canvasboards in the manner of 'Imants Tillers', which he titled *Bell's Theorem* (2002), citing 'Locality Fails', 'chance', 'Gödel', etc., quoting 'possum tracks' from Michael Nelson Jagamara, indeed referencing my first collaborations with Jagamara, which he witnessed in their infancy. The work is dominated by the text:

ABORIGINAL ART IT'S A WHITE THING

That's a catchcry Bell has frequently repeated. Was this a personal message for *me*? *Bell's Theorem* was included in the exhibition held at FireWorks Gallery in 2002 called *Discomfort, Relationships within Aboriginal Art: Richard Bell, Emily Kngwarreye, Imants Tillers, and Michael Nelson Jagamara.*

After this, *Bell's Theorem* disappeared completely from my view until I began writing this text. A Google search on John Bell uncovered a 2014 BBC news report titled 'John Bell: The Belfast Scientist Who Proved Einstein Wrong'.[17] The report revealed a commemorative exhibition for the fiftieth anniversary of Bell's momentous discovery, at the Naughton Gallery at Queen's University in Belfast, the university Bell had attended. The exhibition, *Action at a Distance: The Life and Legacy of John Stewart Bell*, included photographs, objects and papers relating to Bell's work, and videos exploring his science and legacy. It also included artistic responses to Bell's Theorem, 'including a contemporary piece by Aboriginal artist Richard Bell that is on show in Europe for the first time'.[18] I was quite taken aback. But then it dawned on me that I, too, was in this exhibition and *my inclusion had happened without my knowledge*. It was not just the direct references to me in Bell's painting. This was a painting by Imants Tillers executed by Richard Bell. It's now part of my *Book of Power* and has been allocated numbers 99,826 to 99,850.

There is a beautiful text by German philosopher Martin Heidegger in his *The History of Beyng*. It is on 'pure finding':

> Creative finding is not thinking up, is not calculative figuring out, is not forcing, but rather finding one's way into the owned – coming to be that which is *appropriated*.

Being determined through that which attunes.
Without preemptive taking away in advance; without the going ahead of procedure.
Seeking on the basis of *pure finding.*
Coming upon it.[19]

This is also the secret behind Marcel Duchamp's 'ready-mades'. His 'ready-mades' have nothing to do with a conscious act of nomination. Nothing to do with conscious intention. The contemporary art world is awash with so-called 'readymades' and pseudo 'ready-mades': COMPOUNDED OF RAW STUPIDITY. They are everywhere – in biennales all over the world. Artists of all persuasions are busy nominating this or that as art in the most banal misapprehension and misinterpretation of Duchamp's legacy.

In the *Green Box*, the notes and projects for *The Large Glass*, Duchamp writes:

Specifications for 'Readymades'.
by planning for a moment to come (on such a day, such a date such a minute), '*to inscribe* a readymade' – The readymade can later be looked for. – (with all kinds of delays)
The important thing then is just this matter of timing, this snapshot effect, like a speech delivered on no matter what occasion but *at such and such an hour*. It is a kind of rendezvous.[20]

It is true that each of us goes towards and reaches the place he or she can; but not to appreciate the layers of meaning, not to go beyond a superficial reading of Duchamp's 'ready-mades' or de

Chirico's stylistic *non sequiturs,* is to miss the point. And yet with Duchamp, de Chirico and Arakawa, I nevertheless still had doubts. Maybe uncertainty is the only certainty. For *what shall I love if not the enigma*?

Notes

1 Shusaku Arakawa and Madeline Gins, *Mechanismus der Bedeutung*, Verlag F. Bruckmann, Munich, 1971.

2 Michael Govan, in Shusaku Arakawa and Madeline Gins, *Reversible Destiny*, exhibition catalogue, Guggenheim Museum SoHo, New York, 1997, p. 9.

3 Arthur C. Danto, 'Arakawa: (1936–2010)', *Artforum International*, New York, September 2010.

4 Illustrated in the exhibition catalogue *Constructing the Perceiver – Arakawa: Experimental Works,* National Museum of Modern Art, Tokyo, 1991, p. 19.

5 Unpublished text sent to Murray Bail in Sydney.

6 Claudio Bruni Sakraischik (ed.), *Catalogo Generale Giorgio de Chirico*, Electa Editrice, Venice, undated.

7 Giorgio de Chirico, cited in the press release for the exhibition *Revolt of the Sage*, Blain/Southern Gallery, London 2016.

8 Ian McLean, *Rattling Spears*, Reaktion Books, London, 2016.

9 Ian McLean, 'House of Dreams: A Conversation Between Western Desert Painting and Giorgio de Chirico', preliminary draft for essay published in *Dreamings: Aboriginal Australian Art Meets de Chirico,* Carlo Bilotti Museum, Rome, 2014.

10 Murray Bail, 'De Chirico's Future', *Surrealism: Revolution by Night*, exhibition catalogue, National Gallery of Australia, Canberra, 1993, p. 74.

11 Reprinted in this volume, pp. 1–12.

12 Italo Calvino, cited in Georges Perec, *Species of Spaces and Other Pieces*, Penguin Books, London 1997, p. 80.

13 Antonella Sbrilli, 'Album di Ebdòmero', *De Chirico e il museo*, National Gallery of Modern Art, Rome, 2008, p. 47.

14 H. Dukas and B. Hoffman (eds), *Albert Einstein: The Human Side*, Princeton University Press, Princeton, NJ, 1979.

15 Howard Wiseman, 'Bell's Theorem Still Reverberates', *Nature*, vol. 510, 24 June 2014, p. 467.

16 Graham Coulter-Smith, *The Postmodern Art of Imants Tillers: Appropriation en abyme, 1971–2001,* Fine Art Research Centre, Southampton Institute with Paul Holberton Publishing, London, 2002.

17 Greg McKevitt, 'John Bell: The Belfast Scientist Who Proved Einstein Wrong', *BBC.com*, 4 November 2014, www.bbc.com/news/uk-northern-ireland-29904682; accessed 15 February 2017.

18 McKevitt.

19 Martin Heidegger, *The History of Beyng*, trans. by William McNeill and Jeffrey Powell, Indiana Press, Bloomington, 2015, p. 146.

20 Marcel Duchamp, *The Essential Writings of Marcel Duchamp*, Michel Sanouillet and Elmer Peterson (eds), Thames and Hudson, London, 1975, p. 32.

First published in Art & Australia, *Melbourne, Winter, 2017.*

Journey to Nowhere
2018

Counting to infinity

'That the number must rule, that the imperative must be: "count!" – who doubts this today?' Thus writes Alain Badiou in his book *Number and Numbers* (1990). As Badiou points out, 'number' governs every part of contemporary life: economics, politics, science, art. Think of political opinion polls, GDP figures, stock exchange falls or rises, the census, voting for the Eurovision Song Contest, magazine circulations, art gallery attendances, football scores, auction prices for works of art. The list is endless, with the use of numbers representing a claim for objectivity beyond mere opinion. Badiou declares that 'number' even informs our souls: 'What is it to exist, if not to give a *favourable account* of oneself? In America, one starts by saying how much one earns, an identification that is at least honest.'[1]

So I have to confess, that when I started to work on canvasboard panels in 1981, I also began to *count* the panels consecutively with a view to continuing indefinitely. What a preposterous idea! And yet thirty-six years later I have exceeded 100,000.[2] At my modest milestone I don't feel happiness or a sense of achievement but rather a degree of exhaustion at the path behind me, and also the one still ahead. The lassitude of the infinite! But all is not what it seems. When I began my so-called 'canvasboard project' I had been painting and drawing on them, and the idea was that my large wall pieces, made up of a configuration of canvasboards, (for example, in a 7 x 7 grid) would be able to stand alone but also be part of what I have called the *Book of Power* (1981–), an accumulating and evolving entity that would consist of all the canvasboard panels I would paint after 1981. Six years after embarking on this aesthetic expedition I wrote: 'I like to think of my work in terms of a huge all-encompassing book where each canvasboard panel is a page in the book.'[3] The idea comes from the French poet Mallarmé, who wrote in 1895: 'Everything in the world exists to end up in a book.'[4] Furthermore, I added, 'All modes of art can be accommodated within this book, and all modes of expression: from the trivial to the serious, the banal to the profound, the pious to the blasphemous, etc. My intention is the exhaustion of all possible categories.' And perhaps I condemned myself to an endless task when I declared: 'I'll spend the rest of my life working towards this goal.'[5] A statement like this could not have been written without my early interest in, and background as a practitioner of, conceptual art. It is maybe reminiscent of the work *Variable Piece #70 (In Process) Global* (1971) by the seminal American conceptual artist Douglas Huebler, in which he intends to document 'everyone alive'. Huebler sets out the following parameters:

Throughout the remainder of the artist's lifetime he will photographically document, to the extent of his capacity, the existence of everyone alive in order to produce the most authentic and inclusive representation of the human species that may be assembled in that manner. Editions of this work will be periodically issued in a variety of topical modes: '100,000 people', '10,000,000 people', 'people personally known by the artist', 'look-alikes', 'overlaps', etc.[6]

In my thirty-six years of counting, however, I have only managed to reach 102,663 – a paltry amount. And does this number actually represent the number of canvasboards I have painted in this time? The answer is a categorical 'No!' For even as early as 1987 I diverged from my initial concept by allowing the inclusion of the vitreous-enamel-on-steel panels, which were being prepared for an architectural project – the interior of the dome of the Federation Pavilion in Centennial Park, Sydney. I numbered them from 11,809 to 13,248 in my *Book of Power*. As I wrote in 1987: 'After I passed a certain point in the counting I realised that other works, not necessarily on canvasboards, could be included in the panel count by simply being assigned a number.'[7] I thought, 'Why focus exclusively on the canvasboard?' The book now accommodates all media, but the canvasboard continues to dominate.

Temporary visitations

As the main material base for my art, the humble canvasboard has some advantageous properties. It is small, lightweight, rigid, portable and readily available. The canvasboard is usually made from primed canvas mounted onto cardboard. The 'Frederix' brand that I prefer – manufactured in the United States and assembled in Mexico – proudly states that it has been 'serving artists since 1868'. All the same, it is worth noting that the canvasboard has never really been a product used by so-called 'serious' artists other than for perhaps making sketches outdoors. It is above all, due to its inexpensiveness, the favoured material base for *amateurs*.

Nevertheless, as has been pointed out by the Chilean artist Eugenio Dittborn, the canvasboard, or the 'carton' as it was known in Europe, was indispensable to the French impressionists as a means by which to capture their subjects *en plein air*. From these outdoor studies they could later work up their paintings on conventionally stretched canvases in their studios. The boards were treated as process materials, as Dittborn writes:

> The *cartons* of the impressionists were painted to become nothing. Unfinished or failed residues, hieroglyphics, hesitations and approaches, they accompanied the painters of the *plein air* in their incursions as *aide memoires*. Brought back they languished there in dark corners in their studios, together with palettes, photographs, tubes of oil colours, flowerpots, postcards, hats, eyeglasses, bottles of turpentine, Pernod, pieces of cloth, walking sticks, pastels, scarves and *letters*.[8]

It must be emphasised, however, that when my imagination was captured by the possibilities of working on canvasboards I was not thinking of Monet, Pissarro, Sisley or any of the other impressionists. On the contrary, when the first canvasboards arrived at my home studio in bulk (several hundred panels, gleaming white in their cellophane packaging) and I made a vertical stack of them, they reminded me of American minimalism – maybe an element from a work by Sol LeWitt. When laid out on the floor in a grid (as white, blank panels) they were like a work by Carl Andre. These contemporary reference points have stayed with me and from time to time I reinforce them by *exhibiting* stacked panels (both painted and unpainted) or by producing floor pieces that pay homage to Carl Andre. In my studio today, moreover, I am constantly setting out works-in-progress on the floor as grids of panels and then stacking them, complete and incomplete, into three-dimensional formations.

This process, though, is generally hidden from view – or rather, the view of the art public. Mostly my paintings coalesce into single entities on the walls of galleries during exhibitions only to come apart afterwards and morph into small stacks of painted panels, a kind of sculpture that simultaneously contains and conceals an image within. For the most part, this is how my works exist in my studio and how I see them. Therefore, I'm continually reminded of the growing physical mass of my canvasboard production and the fact that my *Book of Power* has a very tangible (indeed undeniable) physical presence. When my paintings are fixed onto a wall I think of them as temporary visitations – ephemeral images that are destined to disappear when they become stacks again. My process thus involves a perpetual cycle of condensation and evaporation – not only physical, but maybe emotional and psychological, as well.

There are of course practical advantages to working with the canvasboards, in particular their portability and therefore mobility. The first solo exhibition I had outside Australia was at Matt's Gallery in London in 1983. I exhibited two large-scale works at 25.4 x 38.1 metres each: *Island of the Dead* (1982) and *White Aborigines* (1983). These two canvasboard works were flat-packed, boxed up and posted by regular airmail from Sydney to London. As an Australian artist of modest means who wanted to participate in the international art world, the canvasboard format was a godsend – a way of overcoming the Antipodean 'tyranny of distance'.[9] Eugenio Dittborn, also from the Southern Hemisphere, solved this problem by developing his series of *Airmail Paintings* (1984–), in which images printed, painted, drawn, or mounted on a lightweight material – somewhere between a smooth textile and robust paper – were folded up, packaged and posted cheaply and efficiently to their international destinations, mainly in the Northern Hemisphere.

In both our cases, the practical advantages of the format also influenced the aesthetic form of our art – the medium is not something separated from the 'art' but indeed totally integrated with it. One could say it is even a large part of the meaning of the art. Through working on canvasboards I have since found additional advantages, such as the ability to cut into the image at the top canvas layer with a scalpel without destroying the integrity of the cardboard below. Hence layering and masking have become integral to my painting process. I would go so far as to say that the scalpel rather than the paintbrush has become my most invaluable tool.

'Take one step!'

In 1990 I produced a single work, an installation, for an exhibition at Yuill/Crowley Gallery in Sydney. I called it *The Bridge of Reversible Destiny* after a project by the renowned Japanese–American artist and architect Shusaku Arakawa. My work consisted of a wall-mounted canvasboard painting dominated by two giant letters: the 'I' and 'T' of my initials. The imagery also included rotating cylinders with radiating lines, two of Arakawa's key motifs. Placed on the floor below, sitting on both sides of the wall painting, were assortments of stacks that included completed paintings dating back to 1982 and works of vitreous-enamel on steel. These contrasted with a substantial column of blank, white canvasboards. The installation measured 11.8 x 2.79 x 1.4 metres and it assembled all the panels available to me at that moment from my studio and the gallery stockroom. For this work I numbered all the elements from 21,892 to 29,336, which involved renumbering all the previously 'completed' works. Thus the counting for *The Book of Power* made a quantum leap of 7,445 in one presentation.

Jan Hoet, the artistic director of *Documenta IX* (1992), viewed the work in Sydney and told me to 'Take one step!'. I think he meant that I needed to decide whether I was a painter or an installation artist. But I had already managed to be both during the 1970s with two complex large-scale works of many parts: *Moments of Inertia* (1973) and *Conversations With the Bride* (1975). Paradoxically, my interest in the avant-garde ideas of that time – conceptual art, post-object art, and the dematerialisation of art – had not precluded my persisting with an aspect of painting. For me, these approaches did not seem to be mutually exclusive; rather, they prompted a consideration of what was foregrounded and backgrounded. It is worth noting, moreover, that my persistence with painting avoided the traditional format of a stretched canvas (at any cost) then as it does now. Indeed in the totality of my oeuvre, over forty years, there would be fewer than a dozen occasions where I've employed a stretched canvas!

Another consequence of working on canvasboards was that I could reuse my own panels. Therefore, it was very straightforward to incorporate, wholly or in part, already existing works. In the early days of the *Book of Power*, such recycling was commonplace in my works. This is very much the case with *Pataphysical Man* (1984) and *Heart of the Wood* (1985) in which the recycled panels give detail, energy and complexity to the overall images. Also, by being renumbered, their inclusion accelerates the counting process for the *Book of Power*. The fastest way to accelerate it of course *would* have been to become an 'installation artist' as Jan Hoet may have been suggesting – a succession of renumbered installations, each increasing the count by many thousands, would be far more efficient and impressive than the dozens or hundreds achieved in the more painstaking process of painting panel by panel. Looking back over the last thirty-six years, however, I seem to have been inadvertently following Mallarmé's maxim 'restrained action', for counting is in and of itself not the primary objective of my art.

From the periphery of the periphery

In December 1996, I moved with my young family from Sydney to Cooma, a small inland town in south-eastern Australia, near the foothills of the Snowy Mountains, often the coldest place in the state of New South Wales – a journey to nowhere if ever there was one! Not long after, we discovered that to overcome the unexpected isolation of our new home, we were going to be more frequently on the road to Sydney and elsewhere. To make this time more productive, since I would be away from my studio for extended periods, I began a project that I called *Daily Research* (1996–). The concept was simply that on standard A4 sheets of paper I would make notes that might inform my practice – sketches, musings, extracts from books, photocopied images, etc. I have now compiled over 6,000 pages of so-called 'daily research' (the number of pages represent around eighty per cent of days over that period) and each page has been numbered as part of the *Book of Power*. Here, literally, in this little subset, 'everything in the world exists to end up in a book'.

The mobility of the canvasboard is echoed by the mobility of Antipodean artists. Because of Australia's and New Zealand's geographic isolation from the traditional centres of the art world, artists from both countries have become intrepid travellers. We think nothing of spending twenty hours or more in an aeroplane (like Riga Sprats in a tin can) to reach Europe or America. Yet this is not an attitude necessarily reciprocated by Europeans or Americans. I well recall, following my showing at the 42nd Venice Biennale in 1986,[10] Nicholas Logsdail of Lisson Gallery urging me to move my family to London for, according to him, to work with an artist in Australia was impossible – 'it's *too* far away'. To my Latvian parents, as displaced persons in 1949, this was the very reason to come to Australia. I was born in Sydney in 1950 and spent my childhood on the southern fringe of this fledgling city at a place named Sylvania Heights.

Having survived war in Europe and its aftermath in Italy, the great twentieth-century artist Giorgio de Chirico moved with his wife, Isabella Pakszwer Far, to an apartment near the base of the famed Spanish Steps in Rome, where he lived and worked until his death in 1978. It is now the location for the Giorgio and Isa de Chirico Foundation and an important part of our yearly pilgrimage to Rome. Every day for almost thirty years, either in the morning or early evening, de Chirico would walk out of his studio, onto the adjoining terrace, and take in the panoramic views of the Holy City below. Standing behind a railing like the captain at the prow of his ship, he would declare, 'Here I am in the centre of the centre of the world.'[11]

Every artist wants to be noticed but some are less fortunate than Giorgio de Chirico. Some great artists have had to make their mark despite working in very isolated places, one could say at the periphery of the periphery. (I often marvel at the isolation of New Zealand painter Colin McCahon at Muriwai!) The story of Australian art includes a series of idiosyncratic movements borne of regional and remote places. For all our increased connectedness, there remains something productive in our geographical isolation, hence my journey for the first time to Papunya in Australia in April 2017. I can now declare: 'I have been to Papunya.'

Reaching the pole of inaccessibility

Papunya is a small remote community in the Northern Territory, Australia. The community is made up of approximately 400 people, the vast majority of whom are Indigenous Australians, many originally from Pintupi and Luritja groups.[12] Surprisingly, according the 2016 census, the predominant religion at Papunya (like in Latvia) is Lutheranism, with 78.7 per cent of the population identifying as such. Senior Walpiri tribesman and Elder of the Papunya community, and my long-term collaborator, the artist Michael Nelson Jagamara (b. 1949), is not one of those, however – when I inquired on my visit, he identified as a Baptist.

Papunya is the closest town to the Australian continental pole of inaccessibility. The *Oxford English Dictionary* defines a 'pole of inaccessibility' as: '(Originally) the place in the Arctic that is in the centre of the pack ice, and so hardest to reach by sea; a corresponding point in the Antarctic; (later also) a point in a continental landmass that is furthest from any coastline.'[13] It is in this latter sense that the term relates to Papunya. The idea of remoteness is significant since the incredible Australian art movement known as Western Desert Painting or Papunya Tula Art that emerged at Papunya in the early 1970s produced a monumental cultural shift from the Eastern coastal cities of Sydney and Melbourne, where hitherto most of the significant Australian art had been produced, to the sparsely inhabited deserts of Central Australia and, eventually, to other remote locations throughout Australia. As John Kean recently noted, 'Seismic shifts occur infrequently on the cultural landscape, and works produced at such rare moments accrue mystique over and above their individual artistic merit.' Kean goes on to describe how the very first desert paintings share 'a particular energy that comes from the moment of their creation':

> The meeting of men with differing life experiences, and originating from such a wide swathe of country, would not have occurred in the traditional context. The efflorescence of imagery that struck in the hothouse conditions of the Men's Painting Room – a Nissen hut in the government settlement at Papunya in the Northern Territory – will not be repeated. For these works were created at the time when the epic songlines that connect Aboriginal Australia were first unveiled.[14]

More than forty years later, we can see without doubt that the only original contribution Australia has made to the history of world art in the twentieth century is Australian Indigenous art, which begins with this very same Papunya Tula movement in 1971. The recent comprehensive survey publication *Art: The Whole Story* (2010) bears this out most graphically, as Papunya artists are Australia's only representation among artworks made between 75,000 B.C and the present, from all over the world. Michael Nelson Jagamara was part of the second wave of the Papunya movement and indeed it is his work *Five Stories* (1984) that is featured and analysed in the book. Perhaps surprisingly, my work *The Nine Shots* (1985) also appears as a kind of small footnote to Jagamara's work under the heading: 'Appropriation Art'.[15] The reason is that my painting became simultaneously famous and infamous when I quoted and scrambled elements from Jagamara's original. But what was a mistake on my part in 1985 (the unauthorised appropriation of an Aboriginal image) led later, in 2001, to the beginnings of a long and fruitful process of collaboration with Michael Nelson Jagamara, which still continues today. Some have described this as 'reconciliation through collaboration'[16]. Initially, in the early 1980s, I was experimenting with the then-shocking tactic of appropriation as a means to unpack and explore my position within art's vast history and landscape, but in the case of my work with Michael Nelson Jagamara, it has led to an ongoing and mutual entanglement. Errors, mistakes, are important. As Novalis has written, 'Error is the indispensable instrument of truth. With error I make truth. The complete employment of error – the complete possession of truth.'[17] It is for this reason that I went to Papunya to visit Michael Nelson Jagamara and his family – and took a journey to nowhere.

Finding a land that did not exist

After one journey, comes another. April in Papunya; May in Karosta – such are the conditions, contradictions and opportunities of modern life. Where is Karosta? Karosta is a small Russian enclave by the Baltic Sea on the Western Coast of Latvia near the city of Liepāja – where my mother was born and spent her childhood. My mother decided to leave Liepāja as an eighteen-year-old in 1943, fleeing the imminent advance of the brutal Soviet Army into Latvia during the last years of World War II. She thought she would return after the war, but she never saw her parents again. In 1976, I visited

Latvia for the first time with my wife Jennifer Slatyer. It needs to be qualified, however, that at the time 'Latvia' as such did not exist. It was part of the Soviet Union and therefore did not appear differentiated in any way on world maps. Although Latvian was my first language and English my second, being of Latvian descent in Australia was of such little consequence that I did not register I was bilingual until I was in my twenties. Being able to read Latvian did not help in Riga in 1976, either – all the street signs, directions, and maps were in Russian Cyrillic.

In 1975 my mother's father was still alive and residing in Liepāja but it was impossible for us to visit him (I did speak to him on the phone). Entry was strictly forbidden and the reason, I now know, was that Liepāja was the nearest city to Karosta. Karosta was thus another kind of 'pole of inaccessibility' but one that was necessarily coastal and for the most part invisible, for Karosta was the naval base for the Soviet submarine fleet. In 1976, I had not even heard of 'Karosta'.

I first came across the name of the secret military town in *A Journey to Nowhere: Detours and Riddles in the Lands and History of Courland* (2009) by the Canadian author Jean-Paul Kauffmann. I read this book on my flight to Riga in 2015. It would be my first visit after an absence of twenty-two years. Kauffmann is less interested in present-day Latvia, or the country's wartime occupations, than he is in an ancient Germanic presence: the Teutonic Knights who founded Riga in 1201 and their descendants, who built castles in the countryside including that of the Duke of Courland. Before Kauffmann visited Courland (in Latvia) in the early 1990s he had 'a few vague impressions gleaned from the books: *A Drama in Livonia* (1893) by Jules Verne and a crime novel *Pietr-le-Letton* by Georges Simenon (*The Strange Case of Peter the Lett* [1931])'.[18] Despite its ancient focus, Kauffmann's book also captures the post-Soviet desolation of the newly-independent Latvia, which I also saw firsthand in October 1991 (immediately following Latvia's declaration of independence from the crumbling Soviet Union) and then again in 1993 when the Latvian National Museum of Art invited me to stage my exhibition *Diaspora*.

I was initially interested in Kauffmann's descriptions of Liepāja, my mother's birthplace and the place to which Jennifer and I were denied access in 1976. It was from there, in 1904, when it was called 'Libau', that the Russian fleet embarked for Japan – a journey of more than seven months that ended in a disastrous defeat for the Russians. But it was Kauffmann's description of Karosta, a few kilometres north of Liepāja, which really aroused my curiosity and desire to go there. Karosta was evidence of the once-mighty Soviet Union, now fallen, and a vindication of my parents' decision to leave Latvia for a better life. I remembered how on that 1976 trip to Riga I had felt so grateful to have been born Australian. Kauffmann describes a scarred and haunted landscape:

> Partially sunk wrecks lie offshore, their hulls protruding above the water...Karosta was the Soviet Empire's second naval base, numbering 26,000 men. Before leaving Courland in 1994, the Russians chose to scuttle all the ships and submarines they were unable to take home. Countless warships lie on the sea bottom: it is impossible to know how many. It is even said that nuclear submarines were sunk...The seafront, once scattered with fortifications provides a spectacle of devastation. Casemates, turrets and blockhouses have been demolished but have not disappeared; on the contrary, they

are accentuated, severely damaged and mangled, made all the more monstrous by the incompleteness of their destruction.[19]

When we visited in May 2017 this is also what we saw. And, in the nearby township that we visited – an enclave that remains substantially cut off from the outside world – another of Kauffman's descriptions, of 'dilapidated houses, rows of ransacked buildings' held true, more than a decade on. There, we saw no Latvians, only impoverished Russians. Tsar Nicholas II visited Karosta in 1901, and while there he laid the cornerstone for the one splendorous building that remains among the Soviet ruins: the Orthodox Church of St Nicholas. This was originally known as the St Nicholas Naval Cathedral, built in the distinctive style of seventeenth-century Russian churches: a central dome surrounded by four smaller ones representing Christ surrounded by the four Evangelists. We went inside and stumbled on the smell of incense and sounds of mournful chanting and weeping – a funeral ceremony. I have been to Karosta. Another journey to nowhere.

Following the unforeseen

Thinking back to that first journey to nowhere in 1996, when I moved with my young family from Sydney to Cooma, I remember the matter of a strange and prophetic map. One could call it a 'map of destiny'. It was passed on to me by one of our new friends in Cooma, Charlie Litchfield, in March 1998, soon after we had climbed one of the three 'Brothers' – the ancient weathered remains of volcanic cores that are a significant feature of the Monaro landscape. It was then that I understood that our home, 'Blairgowrie', lay on the fringes of the Monaro Volcanic Province.

The map in question was a homoclimatic map produced by the New South Wales Government Forestry Commission in 1945. It shows the different climatic zones of the Monaro and South Coast regions of New South Wales and, rather bizarrely, links particular places or towns to other places in the world with similar microclimates. Thus Nimmitabel, south of Cooma, is compared to Nairn in Scotland; Bombala, further south again, to London in England; and Candelo, eastward, towards Bega, to Johannesburg in South Africa. Most unexpectedly, Cooma was linked to Guerrero Ciudad in Mexico. That city no longer exists, though there is a Nueva Ciudad Guerrero in its place. 'Guerrero City' was named after the President of Mexico, Vicente Guerrero (1782–1831), and was the capital of the Republic of the Rio Grande that briefly established itself in northern Mexico alongside other independent states in 1840. Mexico was a place very far from my experience or imagination and I had no desire to go there, yet almost immediately, and entirely out of the blue, I would find myself on the way to Mexico *twice* within the next two years: first as part of the exhibition *Five Continents and a City* in Mexico City in 1998, and then again for a major survey of my work *Towards Infinity: Works by Imants Tillers* at Museo de Arte Contemporáneo de Monterrey in late 1999. And just like that, I have been to Mexico City; I have been to Monterrey.

In the 1890s the great Australian artist Arthur Streeton made a decisive move to relocate from Melbourne to Sydney, and was not long after followed by his fellow impressionist Tom Roberts to 'Curlew Camp'. Situated on the northern shores of Sydney Harbour, the plein air painters used the artists' camp as a base from which to explore the bush precinct, producing some of their finest paintings. In a letter imploring Roberts to join him, Streeton asserted: 'The unforeseen is what is beautiful!' In various ways my practice has surrendered to this beauty of the unforeseen, of chance and serendipitous connections. Having done so, my destination, through my own travels or those of my work, appears at any given time to be both nowhere in particular and everywhere at once. Whether the unforeseen arrives as another step in my aesthetic expedition via the *Book of Power*, or a journey that leads me to a new vantage point, the exhaustion of all possible categories calls for endless wandering.

Notes

1 *Number and Numbers*, trans. Robin Mackay, Cambridge, Polity Press, 2008, pp. 1, 3.

2 The current panel count is 113,874.

3 Imants Tillers, cited in Jennifer Slatyer, 'An Interview with Imants Tillers', in *The Australian Bicentennial Perspecta*, Art Gallery of New South Wales, Sydney, 1987.

4 Stéphane Mallarmé, *Divagations*, trans. Barbara Johnson, Cambridge, MA, Harvard University Press, 2007, p. 226.

5 Imants Tillers in Jennifer Slatyer, 'An Interview with Imants Tillers', p. 111.

6 Douglas Huebler in Yvon Lambert, *Actualite d'un Bilan*, Paris, 1972, p. 63

7 Imants Tillers in Jennifer Slatyer, 'An Interview with Imants Tillers', p. 111.

8 Eugenio Dittborn, in *Imants Tillers: Jump* exhibition catalogue, Sherman Galleries, Sydney, 1994.

9 See Geoffrey Blainey, *The Tyranny of Distance: How Distance Shaped Australia's History*, Macmillan, Sydney, 1966.

10 The art critic, Michael Newman, singled out my contribution as one of the five best exhibits alongside Sigmar Polke, Daniel Buren, Frank Auerbach and Christian Boltanski. See Michael Newman, *Artscribe* (September/October 1986), pp. 53–55.

11 In his memoirs, Giorgio de Chirico wrote: 'They say that Rome is at the centre of the world and that Piazza di Spagna is in the centre of Rome, therefore, my wife and I, would indeed be living in the centre of the centre of the world, which would be the apex of centrality, and the apogee of anti-eccentricity.' Fondazione de Chirico, http://www.fondazionedechirico.org/casa-museo/?lang=en (viewed 15 March 2018).

12 Indigenous people make up 76.4 per cent of the population in Papunya. Australian Bureau of Statistics, 2016 Census, http://www.censusdata.abs.gov.au/census_services/getproduct/census/2016/quickstat/SSC70218 (viewed 9 March 2018).

13 English Oxford Living Dictionaries, https://en.oxforddictionaries.com/definition/pole_of_inaccessibility (viewed 11 March 2018).

14 John Kean, 'Friday essay: how the Men's Painting Room at Papunya transformed Australian Art', *The Conversation*, http://theconversation.com/friday-essay-how-the-mens-painting-room-at-papunya-transformed-australian-art-79909 (viewed 5 July 2017).

15 Ian McLean in Stephen Farthing, *Art: The Whole Story*, Thames and Hudson, London, 2010, p. 543.

16 Sasha Grishin made this statement in his review of *The Loaded Ground* at the ANU Drill Hall Gallery, 'A Real-Life Study in Contrasts', *SSMH*, 29 August 2012.

17 Novalis, cited in Robert Snell, *Uncertainties, Mysteries, Doubts: Romanticism and the Analytic Attitude*, Routledge, Abingdon, UK, 2012, p. 119.

18 Jean-Paul Kauffmann, *A Journey to Nowhere: Detours and Riddles in the Lands and History of Courland*, MacLehose Press, London, 2012, p. 53.

19 Ibid., p. 72.

First published in Elita Ansone and Mark Ledbury (eds), Journey to Nowhere, *Latvian National Museum of Art: Riga and Power Publications: Sydney, 2018.*

The Sources
2019

The Duchampian Prelude

Sometime in the year of 1973 I was engaged in the construction of what I called my 'Black Box' – a kind of model of the art-world as I understood it at that moment. It was a work that I was preparing for a major group exhibition, *Object and Idea,* at the National Gallery of Victoria, curated by Brian Finemore, which included six artists: John Armstrong, Tony Coleing, Aleks Danko, Nigel Lendon, Ti Parks and me. It would be the first significant public airing of my work and would occur even before my first solo exhibition as an artist, which was scheduled later that same year at Watters Gallery in Sydney.

I was not making the Black Box myself but had commissioned Cecil Pitman, the director of the architecture workshop in the Architecture Faculty at the University of Sydney, to make it. It was a complex and intricate feat of construction even for such a skilled man, since the drawers for the twenty-eight objects contained within would closely resemble in their form what they each contained, and even the overall shape of the Black Box itself would be of an unusual, unexpected form determined by its contents.

This work, which I subsequently called *Still Life 2,* could exist in many forms and had many possible modes of display. The simplest manifestation would be for the Black Box to be closed. Thus, it would resemble a kind of minimalist object. However, a minimalist object does not have handles attached so it can be readily moved from place to place by a couple of strong young men, as that would destroy the purity of the form. I did not conceive of the Black Box as minimalist sculpture!

Another mode of display was to open the Black Box and reveal the fronts of the twenty-eight drawers, which had a series of drawings inscribed on them related to the shapes and patterning of the objects within. Or the drawers could be pulled out to show through their Perspex lids the objects within. The so-called Black Box also contained a smaller Black Box which had a mechanism for determining the positions of all the contained objects within a given space. And within the smaller Black Box there was also a kind of catalogue, and other elements associated with the presentation of works of art in a gallery context, as I then understood it. Yes, there were many possible modes of display. After being shown in *Object and Idea, Still Life 2 (the Black Box)* was included in my debut solo exhibition at Watters Gallery in 1973 which I entitled *Moments of Inertia*, and was subsequently purchased by the National Gallery of Australia, where, to my knowledge, it has been presented to the public only twice in the last forty-five years.

Sometime during the construction of the Black Box I had an unexpected, somewhat astounding visit from a curator from the Museum of Modern Art (MOMA) in New York (I have forgotten her name) who happened to be in Sydney on some other mission. At the time MOMA was a mythical, almost mystical, institution for me, and New York was not a place I had ever visited – indeed I had at that stage never travelled by aeroplane anywhere – even within Australia – nor had I ever left Australian shores. Who sent her to see me? I never found out. In any case she had no business coming to an Architecture Faculty workshop in Sydney and talking to a twenty-two-year-old architecture student and would-be artist!

I have little recall of our conversation, but I remember that she mentioned the French-American artist Marcel Duchamp. 'Was my Black Box inspired by Duchamp?' she must have asked. But I really knew nothing about Duchamp; nothing about *The Large Glass*, nor anything about 'ready-mades'. The architecture school at Sydney University did not teach its students art history, but the history of architecture and design, and my research for my thesis *The Beginners Guide to Oil Painting* focused exclusively on *recent* contemporary art – minimalism, conceptualism, systems art, land art, performance art, installation art and so on. It made no mention of Marcel Duchamp. I had no sense of the progression of art history in the twentieth century, let alone earlier periods. Now I realise that in its conception and its miniaturisation of full-scale artworks (which were part of my overall concept) the Black Box perhaps resembled (in her mind) Duchamp's *Boîte-en-valise* (1935–41). But even in 1973, five years after Duchamp's death, he and his legacy were not widely known internationally. Few in the Antipodes would have been aware of him.

Nevertheless, after the completion of my installation *Moments of Inertia* and its presentation in Sydney in October 1973, the words of this unknown woman stayed with me and I henceforth immersed myself in the study of Marcel Duchamp. I obtained and read Arturo Schwarz's massive book *The Complete Works of Marcel Duchamp*, and I studied Duchamp's *Notes and Projects for 'The Large Glass'*. I even found Stéphane Mallarmé's revolutionary poem 'A Throw of the Dice will never Abolish Chance' at the Mitchell Library in Sydney and carefully copied the text and typography onto sheets of paper as best I could. (Mallarmé was mentioned a couple of times in the footnotes of Schwarz's book as a poet and writer who was of interest to Duchamp.)

Eventually my assiduous research into Duchamp led to my next major project: *Conversations with the Bride* (1975), which I created for the São Paulo Bienal in 1975. More recently, it was exhibited in Riga in 2018 at the Latvian National Museum of Art as part of my retrospective *Journey to Nowhere*.

In this work I planned to extend, reconfigure or recreate Duchamp's *Large Glass* (also known as *The Bride Stripped Bare by her Bachelors, Even*, 1915–1923) by using some of the principles and methods of Duchamp as I understood them. My work alluded to chance, logic, alchemy, archetypes, magic, mythology, the fourth dimension, and to some of Arturo Schwarz's psychoanalytical interpretations, as well as the compelling writings of Argentinean author and poet Jorge Luis Borges, whom I had also recently discovered.

My use of mirrors in *Conversations with the Bride* I'm sure stemmed from Borges' unforgettable assertion that 'both mirrors and copulation are *abominable* since they increase the numbers of men'. For my own part, in *Conversations* I proposed a kind of Borgesian mechanism which I called 'coupled moments', whereby the passage, or movement, of unwitting viewers through the work actually created the *secret meaning* of the work.

Three years later I produced *A Companion to Conversations with the Bride* – a single explanatory volume which I believe can still be found in the shelves of the library at the Museum of Contemporary Art in Sydney. But I doubt that anyone apart from myself has ever looked at it.

Following the complexity of my first three major projects 'The Black Box', *Moments of Inertia* and *Conversations with the Bride* there was a brief hiatus when I discovered simplicity – especially in the two works *Untitled* (1978) and *52 Displacements* (1979–80). Whereas both *Moments of Inertia* and *Conversations with the Bride* had used quotation or citation as part of the work, this aspect had been subordinated to another process in that in *Moments of Inertia* as part of *Still Life I* recreated – complete with gilded frame – a still-life painting by the Australian artist Adrian Feint. On the other hand, in *Conversations*, I quoted Hans Heysen's watercolour *Summer* (1909) and put it in dialogue with elements from Duchamp's *Large Glass*.[1]

In *Untitled* (1978) and *52 Displacements* (1979–80), however, questions of authorship, originality and the paradoxical implications of mechanical versus *manual* reproduction became the *subject* of the works themselves.[2] But it was not long before I returned to a greater complexity again, the canvasboard works (1981 to the present, and ongoing) which formed part of the unending, so-called *Book of Power*. But it was not necessarily a familiar complexity since 'the same is not the same as the same'.

Apparition on the Serpentine

In June 2018, I found myself on the way to Riga to install my exhibition *Journey to Nowhere* at the Latvian National Museum of Art but we (Jennifer Slatyer and I) first made a short detour to London. We went to London to see Christo and Jeanne-Claude's most recent public art project the *Mastaba on the Serpentine* (2018), and the accompanying exhibition at the Serpentine Gallery. The first glimpse of the Mastaba apparently floating on the Serpentine was truly astounding. It was like a vision, like a dream – an apparition on the Serpentine.

As Carey Lovelace wrote in *Artnews*: 'there is something

quietly miraculous about *The London Mastaba*, Christo and Jeanne-Claude's 600-ton pyramid-like form that glows red-orange and seemingly sprouts out of its own watery reflections in London's Serpentine Lake.' Composed of rows of stacked 55-gallon oil barrels laid end to end, it is a scaled-down version of Christo and Jeanne-Claude's *Abu Dhabi Mastaba*, which has been in the works since 1979. Were it to be completed it would be the world's largest artwork and it's been proposed for a desert in the United Arab Emirates, where the oil-barrel theme seems most appropriate. Furthermore, unlike many of their projects, this one would be a permanent work of art, eclipsing the pyramids in its mammoth dimensions.

In the Serpentine exhibition I was surprised to recognise one of the models of the *Abu Dhabi Mastaba* – I recalled that I'd seen it before in Christo's loft on Howard Street in Soho, Manhattan in 1979 when we had stayed there on our first visit to New York. Christo and Jeanne-Claude had extended their friendship to us, since I had been one of the full-time volunteers on the *Wrapped Coast* in 1969 at Little Bay in Sydney, and as an architecture student, this profound experience had changed my career trajectory from 'architect' to 'artist'. Not any kind of artist but one who wished to keep company with the avant-gardists! At the London opening we again met Christo, (Jeanne-Claude died in 2010), his collaborator and facilitator on the *Wrapped Coast*, John Kaldor, as well as the Artistic Director of the Serpentine Gallery, Hans Ulrich Obrist who had just returned from Riga after attending the inaugural *Riga International Biennale of Art*.

While imagery from Christo has only recently entered my *Book of Power*, some (notably Keith Broadfoot) have argued that fundamental aspects of my canvasboard project may have been indebted to key aspects of Christo's practice:

With Tillers's canvasboards, which can be placed on the wall, arranged to form a painting, or alternatively stacked on the floor to form a sculpture, the connecting formal element is a flattened pedestal that has become mobile. As with *Wrapped Coast*, which was not only a transitory event but made of what should be stable and immobile – Australia – something destabilised and in transit, so Tillers gives to what should be a permanent and constant form – a painting – quite contrary qualities. Even more like *Wrapped Coast*, though, if Tillers's work displays not its solidity but its ability to be easily dismantled and conveniently stacked or better, if its underlying defining form is a *package* – the canvasboards can be parcelled and bundled ready for easy delivery – then it is as though it is the potential transporting of the work, its circulation, its overtaking by the logic of exchange value, and ultimately its exportability, that is on display.[3]

To reinforce the connection with Christo in a more overt way, I then embarked on a new work, *A New World Rises*, consisting of a large canvasboard painting (on 132 panels) which references *Wrapped Coast* (1969), together with a vast installation of hundreds of stacked canvasboard panels. This work was displayed in the fifty-year commemorative exhibition of Kaldor Art Projects (beginning with *Wrapped Coast* 1969) at the Art Gallery of New South Wales in September 2019.

As the German philosopher Martin Heidegger has pointed out:

History is the coming of that which comes and for this reason alone also the past of that which goes and the having been of what has been and thereby also the presence of whatever is passing.

The Question in the Room

Recently among my notes I discovered that I once wrote:

the question is in the room: is there something missing? Yes and it will always be missing. There is no whole self. The self does not exist. Wherever I am, I am what is missing.

Hence quotations. Why not quotations? Therefore quotations! Some fleeting. Some durable. And without doubt one could observe that in my so-called *Book of Power* there is also something always missing – that is, the next work, the next reference, the next source, the next allocated number as it heads in the impossible direction of infinity, never to reach finality or a terminus.

According to the American artist Roni Horn (who incidentally is also present in the *Book of Power*) when 'something is missing' it is as 'a beautiful definition of utopia'. As she asks: 'would you say that if something is missing it is incomplete or would you say it is complete because there's something missing?' In this sense the *Book of Power* is complete at every moment even though it awaits the next addition at every subsequent moment.

In the index at the back of Wystan Curnow's book *Imants Tillers and the Book of Power* (1998), there is the heading 'Keeping count of the artists in the *Book of Power*'. Then as an explanation Curnow adds: 'the list of artists in the *Book of Power* has three levels. Artists in bold have a dominant presence in the *Book* and they recur frequently. Names in italics occur less frequently, while those in Roman font have a minimal presence – usually occurring once.'

The list of dominant artists in 1998 included: Giorgio de Chirico, Georg Baselitz, Shusaku Arakawa, Jackson Pollock, Sigmar Polke, Joseph Beuys, Colin McCahon and Robert Barry. After 1998, artists who scarcely registered, but were nevertheless listed, like Fred Williams, Philipp Otto Runge, Rosalie Gascoigne, Michael Nelson Jagamara, Eugene von Guerard, Brice Marden, Ferdinand Hodler and Albert Namatjira, became quite dominant, especially Runge, Williams and Gascoigne. Also after 1998, textual quotations – words, phrases, sentences from poets, authors, philosophers, friends, my wife, newspaper copywriters – started to become a significant contribution to the *Book of Power*.

Also, some artists and the aforementioned contributors of text who were not even listed in 1998 became some of my most important subsequent sources – for example Stéphane Mallarmé, Novalis, Emily Kame Kngwarreye, Thomas Bernhard, Martin Heidegger, Egon Schiele, Arthur Streeton, Bobby West Tjupurrula and more recently Kenny Williams Tjampitjinpa. Of course, some of the dominant artists up to 1998 continued to have a massive presence, notably Giorgio de Chirico and Robert Barry, whose signature font is employed for most of the words in the canvasboard paintings. However, after 1998, I decided not to keep count of the artists in the *Book of Power* any longer, for I felt it might be becoming too self-conscious and was beginning to influence my choice of sources. I felt they should come to me instead in an intuitive, serendipitous, autonomous way.

The Encyclopedic Impulse

At this point, beyond this volume of essays collected under the title *Credo*, I feel there is *another book to come* and that this book will be an encyclopedia. Already in my mind I have begun to sketch out how this encyclopedia might be made manifest. It would be in the first instance an alphabetical listing of sources, with images and an index with brief explanations, maybe with personal anecdotes about how and why certain images or texts came to be included in the *Book of Power*. In addition, it would be further enhanced if there were something similar to *Wikipedia* entries on each source, subject and image to provide a more complete context to my citations. Eventually I envisage that this book would be like a dictionary of artists and writers, and to be fully an encyclopedia it would require thousands of pages. And then perhaps it would be taking a few tentative first steps in the direction of Mallarmé's *book*, in which 'everything in in the world exists in order to end up in a book'.

Ecce Liber: Behold the Book

'The Book: What did Mallarmé mean by this word?' This is the question the French literary critic Maurice Blanchot asks in his essay on Mallarmé.

> From 1866 on, he always thought and said the same thing. But the same is not the same as the same. One of our tasks might be to show why and how this repetition constitutes the movement that slowly opens up a path for him. All that he has to say seems fixed from the beginning, yet at the same time the similarities are only so on the surface.

Blanchot's subtle and somewhat baffling investigation into Mallarmé's concept of the 'Book' seems to conclude that Mallarmé's celebrated poem 'A Throw of the Dice will Never Abolish Chance' comes to exhibit some of the characteristics which this chimeric but all-encompassing *book to come* would possess.

Gilles Deleuze, in his wonderful study of Nietzsche's thought, compares Nietzsche's ideas about chance and necessity to Mallarmé's and finds similarities and divergences. The following is a selection of some points that I found pertinent to my own investigations:

1) To think is to send out a throw of the dice. Only a throw of the dice, on the basis of chance, could affirm necessity and produce 'the unique number which cannot be another'.
2) Man does not know how to play. Even the higher man is unable to cast the dice.
3) Not only is the throwing of the dice an unreasonable and irrational, absurd and superhuman act, but it constitutes the tragic attempt and the tragic thought *par excellence*.
4) The number-constellation is, or could be, the book, the work of art as outcome and justification of the world. (Nietzsche wrote of the aesthetic justification of existence: we see in the artist 'how necessity and random play, oppositional tension and harmony, must pair to create a work of art'.)

Each element of my *Book of Power* is a throw of the dice. And indeed, as Mallarmé emphasises (in the last line of his masterwork): 'All thought emits a throw of the dice.'

Novalis

I first came across the name of the German author Novalis in the novels of the great Austrian writer Thomas Bernhard. Bernhard's disturbed and tortured characters would from time to time seek redemption, solace and illumination in the thoughts of Novalis. Who is this 'Novalis', I wondered. Then on my sixtieth birthday I was presented with a wonderful gift: *Pollen and Fragments: the selected poetry and prose of Novalis*. Now I know that 'Novalis' was the pen-name of the German Romantic poet and visionary philosopher Friedrich von Hardenberg (1772–1801) who before his untimely death from consumption compiled notes for an encyclopedia of universal knowledge. This small, extraordinary volume contains fragments and aphorisms of remarkable power on an astonishing range of subjects.

Pollen begins thus: 'Friends, the ground is poor; we must strew abundant seed that we might nonetheless reap a modest harvest.'

Needless to say, the form and content of Novalis' writing was ideal for my own project the *Book of Power*, and over the past eight years I have quoted many of his 'fragments' in my own paintings. Two of my favourite lines are: 'infinite distance of the blossoming world' and 'Every individual is the centre of a system of emanation.' Novalis is a kind of literary precedent for my own encyclopaedic impulse which is mainly visual even though it is only now, in hindsight, that I recognise it to have perhaps been in my practice from the beginning.

While the sources for the *Book of Power* are *manifold*, Novalis would be one of the very first entries in my encyclopedia – indeed the previous paragraphs might constitute the start of the entry on him. Below are several examples of what might be the beginning of further entries.

Paul Neagu

I met Paul Neagu, the Romanian sculptor, by accident, in London in December 1975, after travelling to the São Paulo Bienal in Brazil, when I saw his exhibition at an 'alternative' gallery which I visited. It was my first time in magnificent London. The gallery I stumbled across may have been called AIR Space and his exhibition consisted of 'detritus' related to his performance of the work *Gradually Going Tornado*. Neagu was present in the gallery and engaged in conversation. He seemed interested in me and my art and gave me catalogues, photographs of his work, and on my return to Australia we maintained a sporadic correspondence. I was fascinated by his art – he was influenced by the great Romanian sculptor, Brancusi, of course, but also by certain mystics such as Gurdjieff and Ouspensky. I agree with British artist Anish Kapoor when he describes Neagu in his obituary as an artist who saw his role as a 'generator of a philosophical world view rather than a mere maker of things'. Kapoor points out that in Neagu's 'Proposition for a new kind of sculpture' he had an affinity with Fluxus artists such as George Maciunas, George Brecht, Robert Filliou and Ben Vautier. Furthermore, Kapoor notes that Neagu's residual objects 'out of performance' had a 'peculiar tactility that seemed to give them a ritual feel'.[4]

At the time I had not yet experienced the world of the great German artist Joseph Beuys, but I can now see Neagu's affinity with Beuys, who today is still one of my most important sources of inspiration.

Kapoor mentions Neagu's *Hyphen* sculptures – which started life 'as a three-legged workbench assembled somewhat in the folk tradition of Romanian furniture. Quickly Neagu understood the immense metaphysical potential of his tripod structure. From it he evolved a complete anthropo-cosmic view which, in parallel with Joseph Beuys in Germany and earlier, Yves Klein in France, suggested a spiritual remedy for the ills of contemporary man.'

As Kapoor emphasises, Neagu in his art and teaching went very much *against* British taste in the 1970s and 1980s, influencing a new generation of British artists, including Anish Kapoor himself but also other important artists such as Rachel Whiteread and Antony Gormley. He also influenced me and thus there are a number of references to Paul Neagu in my *Book of Power*.

Georges Perec

I read Georges Perec's *Life: A User's Manual* sometime in the early 1980s, maybe in Paris itself. While I have not quoted from Perec's writings directly, he has entered the *Book of Power* by virtue of the fact that he referenced a number of the train stations on the Illawarra line in Sydney in his last unfinished novel *53 Days*, following his sojourn in Australia in 1981. During my childhood, growing up in Sylvania Heights in the Sutherland Shire, I constantly travelled by train on the Illawarra line – notably to attend Latvian Saturday school at Strathfield. So the names of the stations from Sutherland to Hurstville, and from Hurstville to Redfern, are indelibly etched into my mind. Indeed, I have put the names of a selection of these train stations into a number of my paintings. Peter Salmon in his article on Perec, also notes that in *53 Days* references to Australia abound, and mention is made of the Illawarra line:

While students of Sydney railway timetables will be amused to read of a British commando unit consisting of 'five Englishmen, Sutherland, Oatley, Mortdale, Penshurst, Sydenham'; three Canadians, Redfern, Rockdale, Hurstville; one New Zealander, Kogarah; two Frenchmen, Tempe, Como; [and] one Lebanese, Jannali.

Sigmar Polke

Sigmar Polke first entered the *Book of Power* in 1984. In Curnow's index his name is in bold which suggests that even in 1998 he was a dominant source.

When I was in São Paulo in 1975, representing Australia at the São Paulo Bienal with George Baldessin, Polke's work was part of the German representation (together with Georg Baselitz and Blinky Palermo). The Australian contingent, which included myself, my partner Jennifer Slatyer, George Baldessin, Rudy Komon (George's dealer) and Mervyn Horton, the Australian commissioner for the Bienal, not only met him but befriended him. Early each evening we would meet for cocktails (potent *batidas* – a mixture of raw sugar cane rum and fresh lime juice) and Polke would bring a small entourage with him which included the artist Achim Duchow (one of his collaborators) and a group of local Brazilian bohemians (who may also have been drug dealers!).

Polke wrote his Düsseldorf address on one of his São Paulo catalogues for me. (Incidentally they had been banned and confiscated – they were considered obscene.) The address I have recently discovered was:

Sigi Polke
4156 Willich

Gaspelshof
DÜSSELDORF

I now know that 'Willich' was a legendary hippie commune outside Düsseldorf where Polke lived at the time. However, despite the invitation, I never went.

Later, in the early 1980s, Polke visited Australia unannounced, as a tourist – he went to Uluru and other, unknown, destinations. His partner filmed him at Uluru. Perhaps his cordial relations with our group of Australians six years earlier in Sao Paulo gave him the impetus to visit. In an interview for his recent Tate Modern exhibition in London he describes how the encounter with the Australian desert, in Central Australia, changed his work practice. He became interested in exploring unusual materials and substances from which to make art, rather than conventional oil and acrylic paint on canvas.

One such material was radioactive uranium which he brought (smuggled) back to Germany hidden in his checked luggage. An extraordinary feat, impossible to repeat today. So instead of protesting about Australia's mining and exporting of 'yellowcake' as was the case in Australia in the early 1980s in certain artistic circles, he seized the moment and took some yellow cake for himself to use in his art.

Later we walked past each other somewhere at the *Venice Biennale* in 1986. There was a flash of recognition but we did not greet each other. I was representing Australia and he was the artist for Germany. The next day, Polke was awarded the Golden Lion Award for the best artist.

Fred Williams

In May 2011, I dedicated an exhibition, *Nature Speaks* at the Greenaway Art Gallery in Adelaide, to Fred Williams. In the catalogue I wrote the following:

This exhibition is a kind of homage to the work of one of Australia's great artists, Fred Williams. In the 1970s, as a young artist, I thought that Fred Williams had painted the definitive, quintessential Australian landscape. At that time, neither I nor any of my artistic peers wanted to engage with the Australian landscape tradition – we found it conservative and stifling and besides, conceptual art offered a compelling alternative. However, since the 1980s, Aboriginal artists have spectacularly reclaimed and reinterpreted this landscape tradition, inadvertently bestowing a new relevance on Williams' work. In his distinctive abstractions of the Australian bush, which he typically organises into a somewhat chaotic pattern of hieroglyphs, we recognise some kind of arcane language (an 'ur-text') and we see that nature, indeed 'speaks' but not in a language we can comprehend.

In recent years I have been experimenting with Williams' imagery in my own work – of particular interest to me now is his last, somewhat maligned *Pilbara* series (1979–1981). A number of works in my Adelaide exhibition, such as *Melancholy Landscape VII* (2011) and *Thou Majestic D* (2011) drew on this series. In particular they reproduced the line of undulating mountains from his *Karratha Landscape* (1981). In this painting the uncanny regularity of the contours of the mountain (or is it a hill?) reminded me of the very distinctive 'journey lines' in certain Aboriginal paintings and perhaps they suggest a hidden affinity that Williams' art has with Aboriginal depictions of landscape. It is worth noting that the *Pilbara* series was an unusual departure for Williams into the 'outback' – artistic terrain that he otherwise left to artists such as Russell Drysdale, Sidney Nolan, and John Olsen to explore and colonise.

In my versions of Williams' landscape, the location is the Western Desert in Central Australia bearing the names of places such as Papunya, Tanami, Haasts Bluff, Kintore, Jupiter Well and the names of the disappearing tribes of those areas – Warlpiri, Pitjantjatjara, Pintupi, Luritja. I am also somehow reminded of Albert Namatjira and the words of German poet Novalis who observed that 'every individual is the centre of a system of emanation.' Above all, for me, the desert is a metaphor for the self: 'I shall become no more than movement or stillness or an *idea of being* – there is no-one here.' The desert is a *tabula rasa* – a surface on which the writing has been erased, ready to be written on again.

Jackson Pollock

Everything comes to him
From the middle of his field [...]
There he touches his being
There as he is
He is.

Complex, tragic and immensely influential, Jackson Pollock (1912–1956) created large, bold canvases that revolutionised the world of art. He painted his first 'drip' painting in 1947 and by 1944, *LIFE* magazine was asking: 'Is Jackson Pollock the greatest living painter in the United States?' In the process, Pollock even eclipsed the twentieth century's most famous artist up till then –

Pablo Picasso and together with his cohort of American Abstract Expressionists, such as Mark Rothko, Willem de Kooning, Barnett Newman and many others, moved the centre of gravity of the international artworld from Paris to New York.

As Roberta Smith noted in her obituary of Ben Heller, an influential collector and early champion of Abstract Expressionism: 'Mr Heller's sale of Jackson Pollock's *Blue Poles* (1952) to the National Gallery of Australia, then under construction in Canberra, the nation's capital, was announced in September 1973. The news caused an uproar in the New York artworld: in Australia it nearly brought down the Labor government of Prime Minister Gough Whitlam who had to sign off on the $2 million sale.' It was then a record price for a work of contemporary art, in a price range reserved for works of Old Masters such as Rembrandt!

I first saw *Blue Poles* in 1982 at the opening of the National Gallery of Australia and my references to the works of Jackson Pollock began soon after in 1983 as I was beginning my so-called *Book of Power*. Firstly, I quoted from his early surrealist phase – works such as *Naked Man* (1938–41) and *Guardians of the Secret* (1943). Then later around the early 1990s I painted a substantial number of works based on his *Black and White* series of 1951 which were both abstract and figurative. Being a return to figurative imagery (like de Kooning's *Woman* series of 1950) these works were considered a *regression* for Pollock's oeuvre since they were out of step with the powerful rhetoric of *pure* Abstract Expressionism which was marching onwards towards a triumphant victory for American abstract art.

For me the pure 'drip' paintings of Pollock defied exact appropriation with the basic methods available to me, but the *Black and White* series were simpler, more graphic and did not involve the layering of fine complex strands of coloured paint, which were impossible to imitate. So, my series was done using stencils and a scalpel – a technique which has stayed with me ever since. I enjoyed the paradox of how they were produced (in being laborious and time-consuming) yet they still, from a certain viewing distance, had all the spontaneity of genuine 'action paintings'.

The last work by Pollock that I quoted was one of his last major works – *Portrait and a Dream* (1953) and I entered my version (on canvasboard panels!) into the Osaka Painting Triennale competition in Japan in 1993 where it won the Grand Prize.

Colin McCahon

In August 1992, the Stedelijk Museum in Amsterdam opened an exhibition by the great New Zealand artist, Colin McCahon, entitled *A Question of Faith*. In a brief introductory note in the catalogue, Rudi Fuchs, the director of the Stedelijk (almost universally recognised as the great arbiter of taste at that time) hailed McCahon as 'a great modern Master' – a visionary who should be seen 'on the same level as artists such as Jackson Pollock, Asger Jorn or Joseph Beuys'. Or Cy Twombly and Jasper Johns one might add.

As he admits, Fuchs first saw McCahon's works in an earlier exhibition at the Stedelijk in 1996 – part of *Under Capricorn* curated by Wystan Curnow and Dorine Mignot. (Incidentally this exhibition also included my work *Diaspora* 1992 which extensively references McCahon.) As Fuchs writes:

Seeing those dark, visionary paintings was an overwhelming experience. They were mostly landscapes, or images derived from landscape – and some of them were covered with words and phrases. Some of the words I recognised, they were biblical and Christian; others obviously came from Maori legend (or poetry). I did not understand the writing (bold, evocative – like thunder in the sky), but that could not diminish the powerful and inescapable impact of the paintings.

When I first saw McCahon's *Victory Over Death 2* (1970) at the opening of the Australian National Gallery in 1982 it had a profound effect on me as well. Here was McCahon, a New Zealander who seemed to me to be a far more radical and more compelling artist than any of his most distinguished Australian peers such as Arthur Boyd or Sidney Nolan. As Rudi Fuchs and Marja Bloem wrote in their preface to McCahon's 2002 exhibition at the Stedelijk Museum:

McCahon's impact is such today that it is impossible in New Zealand – and to a lesser degree in Australia – to be an artist without taking his work into consideration.

Even the New York art-world star, Julian Schnabel who happened to see McCahon's work in New Zealand in the early 1980s was influenced. His raw black-and-white text paintings, some of which have Christian religious overtones, painted in 1987 and shown in New York as part of his *Recognitions* series subtitled 'Stations of the Cross', bear the unmistakable mark of McCahon. Unfortunately for McCahon and the denizens of the Antipodes, Schnabel made no mention of his inspirational source in the 'provinces' thus perpetuating the long-entrenched arrogance of the centre-periphery mindset of that time.

My work *Hiatus* 1987 was one of the first to quote McCahon and after it was shown in Sydney was quickly purchased by the Auckland City Gallery. Maybe I was the first artist outside New Zealand (notwithstanding Schnabel!) to publicly acknowledge McCahon's greatness? Definitely maybe.

In any case, from that moment New Zealanders embraced me. For example, the National Gallery of Art in Wellington purchased my major work *Diaspora* (1992) in 1996. The New Zealand poet and critic, Wystan Curnow wrote the first monograph on my work: *Imants Tillers and the Book of Power* published in 1998. Also, Peter McLeavey, McCahon's important dealer and publicist, staged three solo exhibitions of my work in the early 1990s telling me (whispering secretly) that he wanted to seamlessly add my work to the canon of New Zealand art. One of his artists, a contemporary and friend of McCahon's Toss Woollaston, otherwise known as Sir Tosswill Woollaston, even purchased one of my large works from McLeavey. Also at this time, Julian Dashper, the enfant terrible of New Zealand art befriended me. He had lots of anecdotal information about McCahon including the location of his mailbox at Grey Lynn and on one occastion even took me on a pilgrimage to Murawai – one of McCahon's sacred sites. Colin McCahon is certainly one of the most significant of my sources. Then and now.

Robert Barry

Something which is very near in place and time but not yet known to me.
Something which affects me and my world but is unknown to me.
Robert Barry

I have been puzzling over these conceptual works by American artist Robert Barry for over fifty years ever since I discovered something called the 'international avant-garde' in 1969 and they are no more clear to me now as they were then.

As Alexander Alberro has noted, in the early days of 'conceptual art', Robert Barry produced an art 'entirely devoid of materiality' using invisible materials such as electromagnetic fields, ultrasonic sound, radio carrier waves, and rare gasses such as neon and argon, radiations, etc. Together with Lawrence Weiner, Douglas Huebler, Joseph Kosuth and their dealer and publicist Seth Siegelaub, 'conceptual art' changed the discourse and direction of the artworld in the early 1970s, even in faraway Australia.

Fifty years later, Robert Barry's art has changed and developed but it is still an inspiration for me. Indeed, I give homage to it every time I assemble a word, phrase or sentence for my paintings since I utilise the distinctive font that he now employs for all words in his work in whatever manifestation it takes – in a book, in a work on paper, in a painting, on a mirror, on a wall or in three-dimension as a sculpture.

It is interesting to note that Barry was included in the watershed exhibition, *documenta 7*, curated by Rudi Fuchs and Germano Celant in 1982 in Kassel, West Germany, and chose to exhibit a drawing/installation on a window in one of venues, the Fridericianum. It featured not only single words spatially distributed over the window but also a figurative image of a tree together with its root-like structure, in keeping with the new zeitgeist. Barry thought his image depicted 'the veins of the tree', its intrinsic energy where there is as much under the ground as above the ground. I remember seeing this work in Kassel since I too had been chosen to exhibit there (also in the Friedericanium) representing Australia as one of the youngest artists, alongside artists who are now household names such as Anselm Kiefer, Richard Long, Enzo Cucchi, Francesco Clemente, David Salle, Sherrie Levine, Keith Haring and Jean-Michel Basquiat.

Despite his status as one of the seminal conceptual artists in the early part of his career, Barry has shown himself to be adaptable and flexible, and from the early 1980s even began to make paintings (albeit monochrome ones with words placed around the perimeter) and thus was able to be part of the so-called 'return to painting'. A recent wall-text by Barry could even be an (unconscious) commentary on this shift:

IT COULD BE IN TROUBLE,
HAS POSSIBILITIES
WILL LEAD TO SOMETHING ELSE,
IS NOT NECESSARY,
IMPLIES THINGS,
COULD BE MISUNDERSTOOD,
WILL PLEASE SOMEONE,
CAN BE OBJECTED TO,
IS PART OF SOMETHING LARGER,
MAY CAUSE PROBLEMS,
WAS NOT ANTICIPATED,
MIGHT BE HELPFUL,
MAY FAIL.

According to the German critic and curator Franz Kaiser, Robert Barry also embodies the important principle of 'disinterested pleasure'. This is the pleasure of doing things just for the pleasure of doing and without any external target in mind like furthering a career or making money. 'Put in a nutshell: while his generation still took disinterested pleasure for granted, my generation [and mine!] has marginalized it in favour of external priorities like making money, becoming famous or saving the world.'

In a sense my entire project the *Book of Power: 1981 to the Present* may also be motivated by 'disinterested pleasure' and hence Robert Barry's work and career have been, and continue to be, inspirational.

Others, Waiting

If I close my eyes, there are many others waiting for inclusion in my book to come – the so-called encyclopedia – or as it was known in medieval times, the *abecedary* or *abecedarium*.

Thus, under the letter 'B' I would like to include Joseph Beuys and relate the story of how I found a book of his drawings in a Munich bookshop last year with several references in the form of images to his one and only trip to Australia in 1982. These included *Bird Hit by Boomerang*, *Opossum Tree*, *Dreaming Gap (Sternklaver Himmel)* and *Ornithorhynchus Paradoxus Platypus* (all from 1982).

In my library now, I have many books on diverse aspects of Beuys' oeuvre. One of the most compelling is by John F. Moffitt titled *Occultism in Avant-Garde Art: The Case of Joseph Beuys* which explores very convincingly the so called 'Beuys-Steiner connection'. Beuys adopted many of his ideas from the anthroposophist, Rudolf Steiner, and even some of his methods of presentation, such as his use of drawing on chalkboards. One of Steiner's most perceptive observations applies to a significant degree to Beuys' works: 'the essential factor is not what is visualised; what is essential is the fact that the visualisation liberates the soul from the dependence on the physical.'

Incidentally, this also applies to the work of the Swedish artist Hilma af Klint, where we don't need to believe in the reality of her communication with so-called 'spirit entities' in order to appreciate her ground-breaking paintings and drawings.

Sometime in 1998, I came across a small book published by Rosengården Förlag, Hölö, Sweden, containing a short introduction by Gurli Lindén on 'the method and intention in Hilma af Klint's work from an esoteric perspective'. The title attracted me immediately and I began to quote it in my own paintings: I DESCRIBE THE WAY AND MEANWHILE I AM PROCEEDING ALONG IT. I also quoted the cover image of coloured concentric circles in my work, *After the Wind* (1999). Then in 2020, Thames and Hudson published Pepe Karmel's landmark book *Abstract Art: A Global History* with the self-same painting as the cover image! Hilma af Klint, as Karmel remarks in his introduction, 'has recently been recognised as a crucial figure in the early history of abstraction'. And this year in 2021, her work has even been exhibited in Sydney, Australia. A Faraway Land – a land so remote.

Also, under the letter 'B' would be a short piece on the 'unjustly neglected' Australian poet, Christopher Brennan, who, against the grain of Australian literature of his time, was profoundly influenced by Stéphane Mallarmé and indeed corresponded with him. And I would not forget my friend Murray Bail who mentors my literary interests and passes on scribbled notes with phrases and sentences on them gleaned from his own readings, which he deems might be suitable for inclusion in my next painting. A very generous act!!

In a recent conversation we were talking about the writings of the great German philosopher, Friedrich Nietzsche (actually he was Polish) and Murray said quite spontaneously: 'Along with other philosophers, Schopenhauer and Hume – Nietzsche was a very persuasive prose writer.' Sometimes the converse is true, that an acclaimed prose writer might also be a great philosopher – for example, Thomas Bernhard, the author of a 'philosophy of doubt'. At the moment I've also been puzzling over the books of Martin Heidegger, whose philosophy I don't purport to understand but I treat his writing – his unique use of language and habits of expression – as a kind of exotic poetry, extracting words and phrases from here and there. Of philosophy itself, however, I know nothing!

Finally, since this is just a sketch to indicate how I might proceed further, under the letter 'C' I would pay homage to my friend and artistic mentor, Vija Celmins, whom I first met in New York, sometime in the 1980s. In December 2018 the San Francisco Museum of Modern Art opened a major retrospective of her work curated by Gary Garrels and Ian Alteveer. It is entitled *Vija Celmins: To Fix the Image in Memory*. The survey features roughly 150 paintings, sculptures, and drawings, including new works created specifically for the exhibition (no minor feat, as Celmins is a famously exacting and deliberate maker who often takes years to finish a piece).

Elita Ansone, the curator of my recent exhibition *Journey to Nowhere* at the Latvian National Museum of Art in Riga, also curated a major exhibition of Celmins' work in 2014. It was entitled *Vija Celmins: Double Reality*.

Vija was born in 1938 in Riga but left Latvia with her family at the end of the Second World War as part of the massive exodus of about 150,000 Latvian refugees (we would call them asylum seekers today), spending time in displaced persons camps in Germany and eventually ending up in the United States with the majority of other Latvian refugees. As Ansone writes: 'the four-storey building where Vija grew up on the main, and also the longest, street of Riga, which now bears the name of *Brīvības Iela* (Freedom Street) was left behind.' It was built by her father Artūrs, planned as a rental property to provide for the entire family into the future. The building is sturdy and remains standing today and is where Vija stayed during the week leading up to the opening of my exhibition in Riga in June–July 2018.

As Ansone explains, Freedom Street forms the central axis of Riga, and every power that has ruled Latvia has changed its name in accordance with its own ideology. It was *Lielā Smilšu Iela* (the Great Sand Street) in the nineteenth century. It then became *Aleksandrovshji Bulvar*, then *Petrogradshoje Shosse* (Petrograd Highway), then *Revolūcijas Iela* (Revolution Street), *Brīvības Iela* (Freedom Street), *Adolf Hitler Strasse* (Adolf Hitler Street), *Ļeņina Iela* (Lenin Street) and then, from 1991, *Brīvības Iela* – Freedom Street once again.

In 1944 little Vija, according to Ansone, was swept up in the tide of refugees: 'I did not understand what was happening; I thought that was what life was like: people crying often, sorrow all around, bombs exploding...But mostly I was afraid that I might be forgotten and left somewhere. Everyone was always in a hurry; walking with big strides and pulling me along, holding me by the hand.' This is how Vija remembers it.

In June last year, Vija came from New York to Riga for my exhibition *Journey to Nowhere*. She helped sponsor the catalogue, spoke at the opening and we (Jennifer and I) spent very special time with her. This included a day at *Rundāle Pils* together with Elita Ansone. The Rundāle Palace was the summer residence of the German Baron Ernst Johann Biron, the so-called Duke of Courland. Designed by the famous Italian architect F.B. Rastrelli and built in 1736–1766, it is the largest and most significant example of Baroque and Rococo architecture in Latvia. The magnificent palace is set within a beautiful and extensive formal French garden.

Vija and I were also special guests at the closing concert of the Latvian Song Festival – *Zvaigžņu Ceļā* ('following the starry path') – the culmination of the week of cultural events celebrating Latvia's Centenary of Independence. This was held in the purpose-built outdoor stadium in a beautiful pine forest outside Riga with an audience of over 60,000 people. The concert featured 16,500 singers from 427 choirs including many from the Latvian Diaspora, from such distant locations as Sydney and Melbourne. It is an event held every five years and it is reputed to be the largest choir in the world. It was an amazing sight to see 16,500 singers in colourful national costumes on stage at the one time and it is certainly one of the most moving events of my life. Begun in 1873 it is the way Latvians celebrate their identity and dignity. UNESCO has recognised this phenomenon as a masterpiece of humanity in its *List of Masterpieces of Oral and Intangible Heritage of Humanity* (2003). We were seated next to Vaira Vīķe-Freiberga, a former president of Latvia who helped negotiate Latvia's membership to both the European Union and NATO, thus ensuring its future security and well-being.

I Am My Own Search Engine

I am my own search engine. As Heidegger says: I go forth into the world: to be enduring; to be emerging; to be abiding; to be issuing forth; issuing forth 'the art'; creating the *Book of Power*. Maybe not 'creating' it so much as setting it in motion and maintaining its momentum: for the *Book of Power* at times seem to have its own autonomy and I seem to be merely its agent or custodian (I hesitate to use the word 'slave').

I go on paths in spacetime. Sometimes I end up nowhere. At other times I can declare: 'I am now here!' For example, in recent times: on 18 August 2018 (coincidentally my father's birthday) I am in Albuquerque in New Mexico. On 23 August in Durango and Silverton and Pagosa Springs. On 24 August heading south towards the fabled Taos on an endless plain, we cross the deep fissure of the Rio Grande. The next day we are part of the audience for the performance of Leonard Bernstein's opera *Candide* (on the centenary of his birth) at the Santa Fe Opera. There is nothing remarkable or unexpected about this – we all navigate spacetime. We had an itinerary and kept to it.

However, my personal search engine is never completely asleep. We also visited SITE in Santa Fe – a centre for contemporary art. There, in an exhibition I see for the first time a work by the Native American artist Edgar Heap of Birds. Unlike most of his indigenous artist peers, Edgar Heap of Birds makes work that is exclusively text-based and thereby distinctively contemporary-looking. For example, one of his works consists of these painted words:

Navajo
Don't you

Know
Love
You
So

For this reason, probably, Robin Klassnik once exhibited his work at Matt's Gallery in London during the 1980s. I have long known Edgar Heap of Birds' name and reputation but now I could see an example of his work. Nonetheless I had to be in Santa Fe at this particular moment to do so.

Then in the sparsely furnished gift-shop of SITE – a few exhibition catalogues and hidden among them a book of writings by Klaus Ottmann. I recognised his name, as during the 1980s he wrote regular exhibition reviews for the Italian art magazine *Flash Art*, which was an essential reference for me at that time. His book is titled *Thought Through My Eyes: Writings on Art, 1977–2005* and contains texts, reviews and interviews with many artists that still sustain my interest today, such as Joseph Beuys, James Lee Byars, Wolfgang Laib, Anselm Kiefer and Enzo Cucchi among many others. There is even a review of the celebrated exhibition *Dreamings: The Art of Aboriginal Australia* held at the Asia Society in New York in 1989. Ottmann's book takes me back to the 1980s when I was exhibiting regularly in New York and to long forgotten feelings, *exciting feelings* of the place, the atmosphere and possibilities of the period which come flooding back to me. Now I am back in the United States thirty years later, not in New York but in Santa Fe when this happens.

Also, in Ottmann's preface I read: 'Lastly this book is dedicated to the memory of Colin de Land, Pat Hearn, Moira Dryer, Paul Taylor,

James Lee Byars and Pierre Restany. I miss their friendship and creative genius.' Both Paul Taylor and Pierre Restany were also my friends and supporters and very important to me during the same period in the 1980s. Thus I now feel a strange personal connection to Ottmann, despite never having met him. And this happened in Santa Fe, New Mexico!

Back in Albuquerque, where we'd been based for two weeks to spend time with our daughter, her new husband and his family, we spent an afternoon visiting the artist Jack Ox who by a strange twist of fate is now also a resident in Albuquerque, less than a mile away.

Jack Ox, who is a petite woman not a large strapping man, is one of those neglected artists that inhabits the periphery of the artworld. I first met her in New York in 1994 when she'd returned to the United States after seven years living in Cologne, Germany. Her work involves 'translating' compositions written in the aural language of music (such as works by Bruckner, Debussy, Stravinsky, Bach) into a visual language. One of her greatest achievements however was unearthing the lost recording of Kurt Schwitters performing his *Ursonate* (which exists somewhere between poetic recitation and music albeit in a radically abstract form) and translating it into a very precise and convincing visual form.

In 1994 she gave me a copy of this phenomenal, amusing historical recording and it formed part of the soundtrack of our family life in Cooma. As it happened Ox moved away from New York to New Orleans and following the devastation of Hurricane Katrina decided to move on to Albuquerque in New Mexico. So now, twenty-four years later, after being together in New York, we meet again in Albuquerque!

Encounter with Yvon Lambert

Then there is the encounter with Yvon Lambert. This happened in the great city of Paris in December 2014. When we lived in Paris for six months at the Cité Internationale des Arts in 1976, the Galerie Yvon Lambert was one of our regular haunts, since the gallery was noted for its avant-garde credentials. Lambert exhibited cutting-edge artists in the 1970s such as Arakawa, Robert Barry, Douglas Huebler, Joseph Kosuth, Art and Language and many others. Decades later, Lambert opened a superior art bookshop which often carried very specialised titles, impossible to find elsewhere, and the bookshop became an essential destination for me any time we found ourselves in Paris. So, on 4 December 2014, arriving in Paris on the TGV from Stuttgart, I immediately headed for Yvon Lambert's bookshop in the Rue Vieille du Temple. There I found a book with a Latvian title: *ORNAMENTU IZLASE* (*The Ornamental Compendium*). It is not so much *me* finding the book – rather *the book* found me.

It is by Jānis Mazulāns and was published in Gotlande, Sweden in 1979. Furthermore, it's out of place in this bookshop – not the kind of art book one would expect to find here. An older man, distinguished-looking but low key seems intensely interested in my find. 'Where did you find that?' he asks. 'In the other room where there are many old catalogues and contemporary art books on special?' 'No, not there, here,' I answer. The man in question I discover eventually is Yvon Lambert himself. He is truly perplexed by my find and almost wants to seize the book from me. Eventually he relents and we have a conversation – mostly about Arakawa and Madeline Gins whom he knew very well long ago but who have both died recently. I can give him news he has not heard until now, but I am unable to answer his query about who would manage their estate. (I believe now that it is Gagosian Gallery in New York.)

Later I reflect on the Mazulāns book – it is self-published in an edition of only 100 and had been published to coincide with a Latvian Song Festival in Gotland, Sweden near Latvia in 1979, at a time when Latvia was firmly under the yoke of the Soviet Union and the song festivals in Latvia were either banned, discouraged or significantly compromised. Since no citizen of Soviet Latvia could travel beyond the borders of the Soviet Union this Latvian Song Festival in Gotland could only have been attended by the diasporic Latvians – the Free Latvians living in exile across the world. I treasure this book since it is an exploration of ancient Latvian symbols used in textiles, weavings, woodwork, ceramics, even on dwellings. Then there is the so-called 'Lielvārde sash'. As a recent publication notes:

> Part of a woman's folk dress, the Lielvārde sash has an extremely complicated woven geometric pattern that changes up to twenty-two times in its approximately three metres of length. Visibly striking and linked to the signs and graphic symbols of other ancient civilisations as far away as Asia, it was possibly used as a ritual protection or story telling device. Many scholars believe that some ancient coded information might lurk within it.

Obviously Mazulāns was captivated by such knowledge and wanted to disseminate it to the wider world. Today I am convinced that the book was left at Lambert's bookshop for me to find.

The Great Algorithm

The *Book of Power* is an algorithm. It has no regard for my feelings or physical well-being. The *Book of Power* has no empathy. No pity.

It is machine-like. It is not me. As Borges notes in his brilliant essay 'Borges and I' – news of 'Borges' reaches him by mail.

The deterioration of my hips is largely due to my faithful service to the *Book of Power*. Decades of repetitive actions (like those of a *shearer* on the Monaro) – almost four decades of stooping, twisting, putting down, kneeling, picking up, carrying, stacking and unstacking over 100,000 canvasboards – has left its mark. THIS IS NOT YOGA. The *Book of Power* is a cruel master.

An algorithm has ruined my hips. I rue the fact that I did not heed Mallarmé's advice instead: 'keeping vigil doubting rolling shining and meditating'.

The American poet Wallace Stevens once wrote: 'Since knowing and being are one: the right to know and right to be are one. We come to knowledge when we come to life, yet always there is another life, a life beyond this present knowing, a life lighter than this present splendour, brighter, perfected and distant away, not be reached but to be known, not an attainment of the will but something illogically received, a divination ...'

And what is the verdict about *my own happiness?* Did I forget to mention that? I'm inclined in this matter to identify with Friedrich Nietzsche's sentiment when he wrote a short poem he titled *MY HAPPINESS*:

Since I grew tired of the chase
and search, I learned to find;
And since the wind blows in my face,
I sail with every wind.

A Sudden Gust of Wind

On 12 February 2019, I thought that I had completed this essay. Several days later, however, in the prelude to a summer storm on the Monaro, a sudden gust of wind blew through my studio and had the final word – it opened several manila folders (containing my 'Daily Research') on one of my trestle tables and scattered a handful of pages across the floor of the studio. Nature speaks!

These happened to be pages I had completed in 2011 when we were on a trip to Europe, before I re-engaged with Latvia. Amongst the most interesting pages were notes made in Cologne on 3 July 2011, where I transcribed some passages from a monograph on the great Belgian poet and artist, Marcel Broodthaers. Particularly page 87,330 in the Daily Research, which is part of The Book of Power. Broodthaers is well known for his engagement with the work of Stéphane Mallarmé and in this book, I found the following: a poetic synopsis (by the poet Broodthaers) of Mallarmé's 'A Throw of the Dice will Never Abolish Chance' (JAMAIS!), and I thought about how these days there are many references to Mallarmé, even in the writings of philosophers such as Jacques Lacan.

Un Coup de Dés (Extract)

Dice Thrown never when even indeed cast in circumstances of
eternity from the depth of a shipwreck be that Abyss blanched
slackwater raging slated glides despairingly even some wing its own
beforehand fallen back from incapacity to trim the flight and covering
what foams cutting back what soars most inwardly resumes the
shadow buried within the deep by this alternative sail to the point of
fitting to wing-span its yawning deep in so far north as the shell of a
ship listed to one or th'other board.

A very impressive, single sentence which captures the essence of Mallarmé's masterwork perfectly.

Then Broodthaers quotes from Lacan: 'Ecrits ... in sum, Mallarméan' (the last paragraph on page 892).

The sole absolute utterance was started by whom it may concern: namely, no throw of the dice in the signifier will ever abolish chance – for the reason, let it be said, that no chance exists except as a linguistic determination however we conjugate it, as automatism or encounter.

To Whom It May Concern: Letters stolen from the alphabet.

And all this was carried by the unexpected gust of wind!

Hello out there, I wonder are you looking curious? Or? –

21 February 2019
'Blairgowrie', Cooma

Notes

1 Both *Still Life I* and *Still Life II* were part of the exhibition *Moments of Inertia*.

2 This is explained in detail by Graham Coulter-Smith [*The Postmodern Art of Imants Tillers: Appropriation en abyme, 1971–2001*, pp. 137–140]

3 Keith Broadfoot, 'Australian Art on the Move: Christo and Jeanne-Claude's Wrapped Coast', *Australian and New Zealand Journal of Art*, 2014, Vol. 14, No. 1, p. 70

4 https://www.theguardian.com/news/2004/jun/28/guardianobituaries.artsobituaries

Acknowledgements

Many thanks to my life-partner Jennifer Slatyer, for her patience, support, and love. It was her idea to collect and publish my selected wirings in a single volume.

Also, many thanks to Olivia Sophia, my Studio Manager, for her enthusiasm, loyalty, hard work and for her invaluable contribution to this publication.

Incidentally, I would also like to thank the author, Murray Bail, who has mentored/curated my reading over many decades and perhaps, inadvertently, made me a better writer than I would have been otherwise.

And finally, my greatest thanks of all to Ivor Indyk and Evelyn Juers of Giramondo for believing in me as not only an artist but a writer as well.

Remember me.

ISBN 978-1-922725-33-2

9 781922 725332 >